THE
CROSS
AND
CHRISTIAN
MINISTRY

THE CROSS AND CHRISTIAN MINISTRY

LEADERSHIP LESSONS
FROM 1 CORINTHIANS

D. A. CARSON

Baker Books

A Division of Baker Book House Co
Grand Rapids, Michigan 49516

© 1993 by D. A. Carson

Published in 2004 by Baker Books
a division of Baker Publishing Group
P. O. Box 6287, Grand Rapids, Michigan 49516-6287
www.bakerbooks.com

New paperback edition published 2004
ISBN 978-0-8010-9168-1 (pbk.)

Sixth printing, April 2009

Previously published under the title *The Cross and Christian Ministry: An Exposition of Passages from 1 Corinthians*

Printed in the United States of America

The Library of Congress has cataloged the original edition as follows:
Carson, D. A.
        The cross and Christian ministry: an exposition of passages from
    1 Corinthians / D. A. Carson.
            p.   cm.
        ISBN 10: 0-8010-2575-3:
        ISBN 978-0-8010-2575-4
        1. Bible. N. T. Corinthians, 1st—Criticism, interpretation, etc.
    2. Holy Cross. 3. Crosses. I. Title.
    BS2675.2.C369 1993
    227.205—dc20   92-21383

This book is gratefully dedicated to
Perry and **Sandy**,
not because they need it
but because they model it.

Contents

Preface

For too long, many evangelicals have viewed the cross exclusively as the means by which God in Christ Jesus achieved our redemption. Of course, no Christian would want to minimize the centrality of the cross in God's redemptive purposes. But if we view it as the means of our salvation and nothing more, we shall overlook many of its functions in the New Testament. In particular, so far as this study is concerned, we shall fail to see how the cross stands as the test and the standard of all vital Christian ministry. The cross not only establishes what we are to preach, but how we are to preach. It prescribes what Christian leaders must be and how Christians must view Christian leaders. It tells us how to serve and draws us onward in discipleship until we understand what it means to be world Christians.

The content of the five chapters of this book was first prepared as a series of four talks (chapters 3 and 4 were developed from one) for the International Council of Accrediting Agencies (ICAA), an affiliate of the World Evangelical Fellowship. The ICAA coordinates several regional accrediting agencies whose purpose is the promotion of high-quality theological education in evangelical institutions around the world.

The series of talks was then revised and presented afresh at the quadrennial world congress of the International Federation of Evangelical Students (IFES). Representatives attended from 108 or 109 countries. It was an enormous privilege to try to expound God's Word to them. In countless private conversations, I learned a great deal from these brothers and sisters in Christ, and I am grateful to God for their steadfastness, zeal, and unassuming leadership.

What you have before you has been revised once again, this time to accommodate the printed page. Although the form of these chapters is an exposition of parts of 1 Corinthians, my concern goes far beyond antiquarian interest. The message of these sections from 1 Corinthians must be learned afresh by every generation of Christians, or the gospel will be sidelined by assorted fads.

It is now commonplace to confess that evangelicalism is fragmenting. To the extent that this is true, it is utterly imperative that we self-consciously focus on what is central—on the gospel of Jesus Christ. That means we must resolve "to know nothing . . . except Jesus Christ and him crucified" (1 Cor. 2:2), in exactly the same way that Paul made that resolution. This will shape our vision of ministry as much as it will shape our grasp of the centrality of the gospel.

I would be remiss if I did not express my gratitude to Baker Book House for maintaining its interest in this series of basic biblical expositions. Is there anything more important than learning to think God's thoughts after him?

Soli Deo gloria.

1

The Cross and Preaching

1 Corinthians 1:18–2:5

[18]For the message of the cross is foolishness to those who are perishing, but to us who are being saved it is the power of God. [19]For it is written:

> "I will destroy the wisdom of the wise;
>   the intelligence of the intelligent I will
>   frustrate."

[20]Where is the wise man? Where is the scholar? Where is the philosopher of this age? Has not God made foolish the wisdom of the world? [21]For since in the wisdom of God the world through its wisdom did not know him, God was pleased through the foolishness of what was preached to save those who believe. [22]Jews demand miraculous signs and Greeks look for wisdom, [23]but we preach Christ crucified: a stumbling block to Jews and foolishness to Gentiles, [24]but to those whom God has called, both Jews and Greeks, Christ the power of God and the

wisdom of God. [25]For the foolishness of God is wiser than man's wisdom, and the weakness of God is stronger than man's strength.

[26]Brothers, think of what you were when you were called. Not many of you were wise by human standards; not many were influential; not many were of noble birth. [27]But God chose the foolish things of the world to shame the wise; God chose the weak things of the world to shame the strong. [28]He chose the lowly things of this world and the despised things—and the things that are not—to nullify the things that are, [29]so that no one may boast before him. [30]It is because of him that you are in Christ Jesus, who has become for us wisdom from God— that is, our righteousness, holiness and redemption. [31]Therefore, as it is written: "Let him who boasts boast in the Lord."

[1]When I came to you, brothers, I did not come with eloquence or superior wisdom as I proclaimed to you the testimony about God. [2]For I resolved to know nothing while I was with you except Jesus Christ and him crucified. [3]I came to you in weakness and fear, and with much trembling. [4]My message and my preaching were not with wise and persuasive words, but with a demonstration of the Spirit's power, [5]so that your faith might not rest on men's wisdom, but on God's power.

What would you think if a woman came to work wearing earrings stamped with an image of the mushroom cloud of the atomic bomb dropped over Hiroshima?

What would you think of a church building adorned with a fresco of the massed graves at Auschwitz?

Both visions are grotesque. They are not only intrinsically abhorrent, but they are shocking because of powerful cultural associations.

The same sort of shocked horror was associated with *cross* and *crucifixion* in the first century. Apart from the emperor's explicit sanction, no Roman citizen could be put to death by this means. Crucifixion was reserved for slaves, aliens, barbarians. Many thought it was not something to be talked about in polite company. Quite apart from the wretched torture inflicted on those who were executed by hanging from a cross, the cultural associations conjured up images of evil, corruption, abysmal rejection.

Yet today, crosses adorn our buildings and letterheads, grace our bishops, shine from lapels, and dangle from our ears—and no one is scandalized. It is this cultural distance from the first century that makes it so hard for us to feel the compelling irony of 1 Corinthians 1:18: "For the message of the cross is foolishness to those who are perishing, but to us who are being saved it is the power of God."

Yet this cultural distance must be bridged. We must return again and again to the cross of Jesus Christ if we are to take the measure of our Christian living, our Christian service, our Christian ministry.

To begin at the beginning, I want to trace the place of the cross in Christian preaching and Christian proclamation. It will be helpful to follow the theme in three parts, corresponding to the three principal paragraphs in our biblical text.

The Message of the Cross (1:18–25)

Paul has already criticized the Corinthians for their divisive spirit. One party says, "I follow Paul"; another, "I follow Apollos"; another, "I follow Cephas"; yet another, probably the most sanctimonious of the lot, "I follow Christ" (1:11–12). Both of Paul's letters to the Corinthians demonstrate that believers in that city were constantly tempted to attach themselves to strong leaders and then look down on others. Fascinated by the rhetoric of learned scholars of their day, the Corinthians were sometimes more impressed by form and show than by content and truth. They loved "words of human wisdom" (1:17)—literally, "wisdom of word," the wit and eloquence that neatly packaged more than one school of thought in first-century Greece.

But while many siren voices told people what to believe and how to live, eloquently appealing all the while to the "wisdom of word," Paul simply resolved to proclaim the gospel (1:17), "the message of the cross" (1:18). All his focus is on the content of his message. God was pleased to save those who believe "through the foolishness of what was preached" (1:21). It is the content of what is preached that Paul here emphasizes, not the act of preaching (as some versions suggest: e.g., "the foolishness of preaching" [KJV]).

Paul delineates two critical features in this message of the cross:

The Message of the Cross, by God's Determination, Divides the Human Race Absolutely (1:18–21)

The ancient world deployed various polarities for describing humanity: Romans and barbarians, Jews and Gentiles, slaves and free. But Paul here sets forth the only polarity that is of ultimate importance: he distinguishes between those who are perishing and those who are being saved. The dividing line between these two groups is the message of the cross: "the message of the cross is foolishness to those who are perishing, but to us who are being saved it is the power of God" (1:18).

Indeed, Paul emphasizes that this fundamental distinction arises from God's stated purposes: "For it is written," Paul writes in verse 19, and then cites Scripture. God has already declared himself on this question, so for Paul it is settled.

The Scripture passage he cites is Isaiah 29:14: "I will destroy the wisdom of the wise; the intelligence of the intelligent I will frustrate." In other words, the message of the cross is nothing other than God's way of doing what he said he would do: by the cross, God sets aside and shatters all human pretensions to strength and wisdom.

This is a central theme of Scripture. God made us to gravitate toward him, to acknowledge with joy and obedience that he is the center of all, that he alone is God. The heart of our wretched rebellion is that each of us wants to be number one. We make ourselves the center of all our thoughts and hopes and imaginings. This vicious lust to be first works its way outward not only in hatred, war, rape, greed, covetousness, malice, bitterness, and much more, but also in self-righteousness, self-promotion, manufactured religions, and domesticated gods.

We ruefully acknowledge how self-centered we are after we have had an argument with someone. Typically, we mentally conjure up a rerun of the argument, thinking up all the things we could have said, all the things we should have said. In such reruns, we always win. After an argument, have you ever conjured up a rerun in which you lost?

Our self-centeredness is deep. It is so brutally idolatrous that it tries to domesticate God himself. In our desperate folly we act as if we can outsmart God, as if he owes us explanations, as if we are wise and self-determining while he exists only to meet our needs.

But this God says, "I will destroy the wisdom of the wise; the intelligence of the intelligent I will frustrate." Indeed, the point has already been made implicitly in verse 18. One might have expected Paul to say, "For the message of the cross is foolishness to those who are perishing, but to us who are being saved it is the *wisdom* of God." Instead, he insists it is "the *power* of God." Of course, he will later say that the gospel is also God's wisdom (1:24), but he starts off on a different note. This is not a slip on Paul's part; the point is crucial. Paul does not want the Corinthians to think that the gospel is nothing more than a philosophical system, a supremely wise system that stands over against the folly of others. It is far more: where human wisdom utterly fails to deal with human need, God himself has taken action. We are impotent when it comes to dealing with our sin and being reconciled to God, but where we are impotent God is powerful. Human folly and human wisdom are equally unable to achieve what God has accomplished in the cross. The gospel is not simply good advice, nor is it good news about God's power. The gospel is God's power to those who believe. The place where God has supremely destroyed all human arrogance and pretension is the cross.

Paul drives the point home with three stinging rhetorical questions:

"Where is the wise man?" (1:20). In first-century Corinth, "wisdom" was not understood to be practical skill in living under the fear of the Lord (as it frequently is in Proverbs), nor was it perceived to be some combination of intuition, insight, and people smarts (as it frequently is today in the West). Rather, wisdom was a public philosophy, a well-articulated world-view that made sense of life and ordered the choices, values, and priorities of those who adopted it. The "wise man," then, was someone who

adopted and defended one of the many competing public world-views. Those who were "wise" in this sense might have been Epicureans or Stoics or Sophists or Platonists, but they had this in common: they claimed to be able to "make sense" out of life and death and the universe.

An organizing system, a coherent world-view, conveys a sense of power. If you can explain life, you remain in control of it. The Greeks were renowned for their pursuit of coherent systems of thought that ordered their world. In short, they pursued "wisdom."

But Paul's rhetorical question asks, in effect, which of these public systems of thought disclosed the gospel? Which "wise man" discerned God's marvelous plan of redemption?

In the light of the cross, how well do the raucous appeals of competing public philosophies stand up? What place does the cross have in communism? What place does the cross have in capitalism? Does systematic hedonism lead anyone to the cross? How about dogmatic pluralism? Will secular humanism lead anyone to the most astonishing act of divine self-disclosure that has ever occurred—the cross of Christ?

Does the elevation of the virtues of democracy lead men and women to the cross? In America, the founding fathers conceived of democracy as a way of establishing accountability by restricting power. If the populace as a whole did not like the executive, legislative, or judicial branches of government, the ballot box provided a means of turfing them out. Strangely, modern politicians speak of "the wisdom of the American people," as if special insight resides in the masses. That was not the perception of the founding fathers; it is certainly not a Christian evaluation. Doubtless, democracy is the best form of government where the populace is reasonably literate and shares many common values, but even under these conditions the majority vote does not always display great wisdom. It is the best way to limit power and make government more or less responsive; it is not the best way of determining right and wrong, truth and falsehood, good and bad. Does democracy itself lead anyone to the cross? Is it not always wrong to equate "the American way," or, more broadly, any democratic system, with the gospel?

Paul's point is that no public philosophy, no commonly accepted "wisdom," can have enduring significance if its center is not the cross. Whatever the merits or the demerits of these various systems, they exhaust their resources on merely superficial levels. They do not reconcile men and women to the living God, and nothing is more important than that. They cannot uncover God's wisdom in the cross, and if that is hidden all other "wisdom" is foolish. Where is the wise man?

"Where is the scholar?" (1:20). The rendering *scholar* is misleading. *Scholar* suggests an academic, perhaps a very gifted one. The Greek word *grammateus* used here was not used in Greek culture to denote any kind of advanced scholar. What Paul has in mind is the use of the term among Greek-speaking Jews: the *grammateus* was the "scribe," the expert in the law of God, the person knowledgeable in biblical heritage and in all the tradition that flowed from it. Thus, in his first two rhetorical questions Paul anticipates both the Greeks who look for wisdom and the Jews who seek miraculous signs (1:22).

Paul's point here, then, is that theologians, biblical experts, ethicists, and the ancient equivalent of ecclesiastics fared no better than the "wise man." None of them had developed a system where the cross stands at the very center; none of them had anticipated "good news" from God that would make much of the odious death of the long-awaited Messiah. With even less excuse, our generation multiplies religious sentiment long on "self-fulfillment" and "personal need" and painfully short of thoughtful examination of what it cost Almighty God to pursue rebellious human beings and win them to himself.

"Where is the philosopher of this age?" (1:20). The word rendered "philosopher" might more literally be translated "debater" or "orator." But in Greek culture rhetoric was so highly regarded that the best public philosophers were almost inevitably gifted and trained rhetoricians. To them, form was as important as content.

But where were these philosophers and debaters when Jesus was dying on the cross? How well did their infatuation with form prepare them to follow one who never danced to faddish tunes? No matter how celebrated they were as they mastered the media of their day and earned sheaves of laurels for their brilliant performances, they were blind and lost when it came to what is of transcendental importance.

The plain fact of the matter is that in the cross God has "made foolish the wisdom of the world" (1:20). Paul does not merely mean that God made the world's wisdom appear to be foolish. What he says is far stronger: God has made foolish the wisdom of the world. He has reduced the vaunted wisdom of the world to folly. He has pricked its pretensions and established its foolishness. How has God done this?

In the first place, Paul says, the utter bankruptcy of all the world's efforts to know God was part of God's wise design. It was "in the wisdom of God" that "the world through its wisdom did not know him" (1:21). Not only did the wise and the scholars and the philosophers fail to understand, God in his all-wise providence actually worked it out that way. Their failures are thoroughly blameworthy; their ignorance of God and their endless, self-centered preoccupation are culpable. Nevertheless, no evil, certainly not theirs, can escape the bounds of God's sovereign providence—and it is God himself who ensures that the world in its wisdom does not know him. It is not hard to see why: in this fallen order, human "wisdom" (in the sense already described) is deeply idolatrous. How can idolatrous attempts to domesticate God be rewarded with deepening knowledge of the Almighty? It could never be! God himself has ensured that it cannot be. And thus God himself has established the utter folly of this world's wisdom.

There is a second way in which God has "made foolish the wisdom of the world." Granted that through God's wise providence the world has not known him, God determined that some men and women would come to know him—but through a means utterly unexpected and unforeseen by the "wise" people of the world. "God was pleased through the foolishness of what was preached to save those who believe" (1:21).

We need to think about this statement very carefully. The New International Version's translation here is basically right: God determined to save those who believe "through the foolishness of what was preached," not "by the foolishness of preaching" (KJV)—as if there were something inherently transforming in the act of preaching. The focus, as we have seen, is on the content of the preaching, not the form.[1] The content of "what was preached" Paul goes on to stipulate in verse 23, still to be explored. Quite simply, it is "Christ crucified." That notion is not something that the world, despite its vaunted wisdom, would ever have thought up. But God abases the world's pretensions still more; he determines that the message of the cross, the content of what is preached, should save "those who believe."

This is breathtaking. God has not arranged things so that the foolishness of the gospel saves those who have IQs in excess of 130. Where would that leave the rest of us? Nor does the foolishness of what is preached transform the young, the beautiful, the extroverts, the educated, the wealthy, the healthy, the upright. Where would that leave the old, the ugly, the introverts, the illiterate, the poor, the sick, the perverse?

The gods of the rich are not gentle with those the rich dismiss as poor; the gods of the wise are not kind to those the wise reject as stupid; the gods of the social elite are not patient with outcasts.

Granted that this is a fallen, rebellious world, the gods that are "discovered" (should we not rather say invented?) by human wisdom are mere projections of our hubris. But the true God, the God who is there (as Francis Schaeffer used to say), dismisses them all. He has "made foolish the wisdom of the world" (1:20); he has been pleased to save "those who believe." These people are saved by him, not because he chooses those who boast some superior trait or insight, not because he loves people who judge themselves to be wise, but because he has determined to rescue those who believe him. By his grace, they trust him, they rely on him, they abandon themselves to him. He is their center, their rock, their hope, their anchor, their confidence. And thus God quietly and effectively banishes the wisdom of our culture as utter folly.

Thus the message of the cross divides the human race absolutely: it is "foolishness to those who are perishing, but to us who

---

1. Of course, even the NIV talks about "the foolishness of what was *preached*," not "the foolishness of what was *discussed* or *shared*" or the like. The significance of Paul's choice of language will be explored later in this chapter, when 2:1–5 is expounded.

are being saved it is the power of God" (1:18). On the one side are those whose religion, or lack of it, seeks a domesticated God accessible to the informed, the initiated, the wise; on the other side are those who have received the foolishness of the gospel by faith and are saved.

Paul stresses a second element in the message of the cross:

The Message of the Cross Proves That God's Folly Has Outsmarted Human Wisdom; His Weakness Has Overpowered Human Strength (1:22–25)

Paul now divides those who are perishing into two groups. These two groups represent the fundamental idolatries of his age, and of every age:

"Jews demand miraculous signs" (1:22). Historically, of course, this is what happened to Jesus on more than one occasion. When "some of the Pharisees and teachers of the law said to him, 'Teacher, we want to see a miraculous sign from you,'" he replied, "A wicked and adulterous generation asks for a miraculous sign!" (Matt. 12:38–39). They were openly testing him by demanding a sign (Matt. 16:1). Even those who out of sheer desperation asked Jesus for miraculous help could at first be gently rebuffed, with words such as these, "Unless you people see miraculous signs and wonders . . . you will never believe" (John 4:48). In some cases, such as the feeding of the five thousand, Jesus' miraculous power was attractive to the crowd simply because of what it gave them (John 6:26).

But one might well ask why Jesus should object. After all, he performed many miracles. Why should he object when someone asked him for one? Did not such requests simply give him an opportunity to display yet one more powerful work?

These questions miss the point. There is a kind of longing for a display of Jesus' power that is entirely godly, submissive, perhaps even desperate. There is another kind that puts the person making the request into the driver's seat. Some want to see Jesus perform a sign so that they can evaluate him, assess his claims, test his credentials. At one level, of course, he accommodates himself to our unbelief by performing miracles that ought to elicit faith (John 10:38). But at another level, he cannot possibly reduce himself to nothing more than a powerful genie who performs spectacular tricks on command. As long as people are assessing him, they are in the superior position, the position of judge. As long as they are checking out his credentials, they are forgetting that God is the one who will weigh them. As long as they are demanding signs, Jesus, if he constantly acquiesces, is nothing more than a clever performer.

Thus the demand for signs becomes the prototype of every condition human beings raise as a barrier to being open to God. I will devote myself to this God *if* he heals my child. I will follow this Jesus *if* I can maintain my independence. I will happily become a Christian *if* God proves himself to me. I will turn from my sin and read the Bible *if* my marriage gets sorted out to my satisfaction. I will acknowledge Jesus as Lord *if* he performs the kind of miracle, on demand, that removes all doubt. In every case, I am assessing him; he is not assessing me. I am not coming to him on his terms; rather, I am stipulating terms that he must accept if he wants the privilege of my company. "Jews demand miraculous signs."

"Greeks [i.e., Gentiles] look for wisdom" (1:22). We have already discovered what this means. These people may not erect conditions that God has to meet, but they do something just as bad. They create entire structures of thought so as to maintain the delusion that they can explain everything. They think they are scientific, in control, powerful. God, if he exists, must meet the high standards of their academic and philosophical prowess and somehow fit into their system, if he is to be given any sort of respectful hearing.

In both "Jews" and "Greeks," there is profound self-centeredness. God is not taken on trust. Both the demand for signs and the pursuit of "wisdom," and all the countless progeny they have spawned, treat God as if we have the right to approve him, to examine his credentials. This is the most reprehensible wickedness, the most appalling insolence, the most horrific mark of our deep rebellion and lostness.

By contrast, Paul says, "we preach Christ crucified" (1:23). That is our content, and to those who do not know Christ it is an astonishingly odd message. In the first century, it must have sounded like a contradiction in terms, like frozen steam or hateful love or upward decline or godly rapist—only far more shocking. For many Jews, the long-expected Messiah[2] had to come in splendor and glory; he had to begin his reign with uncontested power. "Crucified Messiah": this juxtaposition of words is only a whisker away from blasphemy, since every Jew knows that God himself has declared that everyone who hangs in shame on a tree stands under God's curse (Deut. 21:23). How could God's Messiah be under God's curse? How could God's Messiah be crucified? To the Jew, the very idea is a "stumbling block" (1:23), the ultimate scandal. That is what Paul himself thought before he was converted. He was outraged that fellow Jews should honor as Messiah, indeed as God himself, a man whom God had obviously cursed (see Gal. 1:13–14; 3:13).

But Greeks could not regard "Christ crucified" any more highly. They exalted reason and public philosophy, not faith and public criminals. Not many years would elapse before Emperor Trajan would dismiss Christianity as a "pernicious superstition"—and he was simply articulating widely held opinion. More broadly, Romans more interested in power than in philosophy would dismiss an expression like "crucified hero" as utter foolishness (1:23). Perhaps that is why Paul subtly moves from describing "Greeks" (v. 22) to mentioning "Gentiles" (v. 23). He wants to make it clear that the cross is foolishness not only to Greeks but to all Gentiles, that no one is left out, that the cross is scandal or folly to everyone. Even the word Paul uses for "foolishness" is not accidental; it can be understood to mean "mania" or "madness." Gentiles wrote off the message of the cross not as eccentric, harmless folly, but as dangerous, almost deranged, stupidity.

The cross, then, is dismissed and derided by everyone. But still, Paul insists, "we preach Christ crucified" (1:23). The message of the cross may be nonsense to those who are perishing, "a stumbling block to Jews and foolishness to Gentiles" (1:23), "but to those whom God has called, both Jews and Greeks, Christ the power of God and the wisdom of God" (1:24).

This is an astonishing claim!

We will better feel its power if we note two things. First, those who stand apart from the perishing world are "those whom God

---

2. Messiah and Christ are equivalent, the former springing from a Hebrew background and the latter from Greek.

has called." The fundamental reason they are different is that God has called them—which in Paul's use means that God has reached out and saved them. God's "call," as Paul refers to it, is effective: those whom God calls are inevitably converted (see Rom. 8:30). True, these same people can be referred to as "those who believe" (1:21). From the human perspective, faith appropriates the peerless benefits of Christ's cross. But the question of ultimate cause must be asked: If it was God's wisdom that ensured that the world through its wisdom would not know him (1:21), how did these people come to believe? If everyone finds the cross foolish and repulsive, how did these people come to delight in it? Paul's answer: They were called by God himself (1:24)—a point he reiterates a couple of verses later.

Second, these God-called people, "both Jews and Greeks" (i.e., people called by God without racial distinction), have come to discover that Christ, Christ crucified, is "the power of God and the wisdom of God" (1:24). The language is chosen carefully. The Jews demanded powerful signs and expected a powerful Messiah. They were offended at the ridiculous implausibility and inherent weakness of any notion of "Messiah crucified." Yet in deep irony, it is that moment of sublime weakness, the cross of Jesus Christ, that most greatly displays the power of God— and Christians recognize it. For their part, the Gentiles loved what they called wisdom. They dismissed as crass foolishness any notion of a hero who was crucified. Yet in deep irony, it is this moment of transparent folly, the cross of Jesus Christ, that most greatly displays God's breathtaking wisdom. That is what Paul says: "to those whom God has called," regardless of background, Christ crucified is "the power of God and the wisdom of God" (1:24).

This is both deliciously ironic and entirely appropriate. It is ironic because what the world dismisses with a shudder is nothing less than God's means of bringing blessing the world cannot otherwise obtain. It is appropriate because all of the world's rebellious self-centeredness is precisely what ensures that it cannot understand the cross, while God's wise plan of redemption hinges on God himself taking self-denying action to bring about the consummation of his authority.

Paul did not come by this insight easily. For him, it began on the Damascus road. When he came face to face with the resurrected and glorified Jesus whom he had dismissed as a shameful usurper who deserved the curse of God that fell on him, he had to revise many of the structures of his thought. If Jesus was alive, then the Christians who kept insisting they were witnesses of the resurrection had to be listened to with new respect. If Jesus was alive, and glorified, then God could not have placed an irrevocable curse on him. But if the meaning of the cross was not that Jesus was doomed under God's curse, what was its meaning? If Jesus' resurrection proved that Jesus was vindicated by God himself, even though he had died in shame on the odious cross, what was the significance of that death?

Only the Christian claim made sense. Jesus was the promised Messiah, all right, but he was also the suffering Servant. Certainly he was the reigning King who claimed that all authority was his, but he was also the fulfillment of multiplied centuries of bloody sacrifices, all pointing forward to the supreme sacrifice which alone could effectively deal with sin. Jesus died under God's curse, all right, not on account of his own sin, but on account of mine. And the value of his sacrifice is most spectacularly vindicated in the most remarkable fact of history: God raised him from the dead.

Called of God, Christians have always fastened their confidence to the cross of Jesus Christ. That is why we still sing, for instance, this hymn from the Middle Ages:

> O sacred head! sore wounded,
>   With grief and shame bowed down,
> Now scornfully surrounded
>   With thorns, Thy only crown!
> How pale art Thou with anguish,
>   With sore abuse and scorn!
> How does that visage languish,
>   Which once was bright as morn!
>
> What Thou, my Lord, hast suffered,
>   Was all for sinners' gain:
> Mine, mine was the transgression,
>   But Thine the deadly pain:
> Lo! here I fall, my Saviour;

'Tis I deserve Thy place;
Look on me with Thy favour,
Vouchsafe to me Thy grace.

What language shall I borrow
To thank Thee, dearest friend,
For this, Thy dying sorrow,
Thy pity without end?
O make me Thine for ever;
And should I fainting be,
Lord, let me never, never
Outlive my love to Thee!

Be near me when I'm dying,
O show Thy cross to me,
And, for my succour flying,
Come, Lord, and set me free!
These eyes, new faith receiving,
From Jesus shall not move;
For he who dies believing,
Dies safely through Thy love.

Bernard de Clairvaux (1090–1153)

What the world dismisses as sheer foolishness, the foolishness of God, proves "wiser than man's wisdom" (1:25). What the world writes off as hopeless weakness, the weakness of God, proves "stronger than man's strength" (1:25). This is much more radical than saying that God has more wisdom than human beings, or that he is stronger than human beings—as if we are dealing with mere degrees of wisdom and power. No, we are dealing with polar opposites. Human "wisdom" and "strength" are, from God's perspective, rebellious folly and moral weakness. And the moment when God most dramatically discloses his own wisdom and strength, the moment when his own dear Son is crucified— although it is laughed out of court by the tawdry "wisdom" of this rebellious world, by the pathetic "strength" of the self-deceived— is nevertheless the moment of divine wisdom and divine power. "For the foolishness of God is wiser than man's wisdom, and the weakness of God is stronger than man's strength" (1:25).

For those of us in any form of Christian ministry, this lesson must constantly be reappropriated. Western evangelicalism tends to run through cycles of fads. At the moment, books are pouring off the presses telling us how to plan for success, how "vision" consists in clearly articulated "ministry goals," how the knowledge of detailed profiles of our communities constitutes the key to successful outreach. I am not for a moment suggesting that there is nothing to be learned from such studies. But after a while one may perhaps be excused for marveling how many churches were planted by Paul and Whitefield and Wesley and Stanway and Judson without enjoying these advantages. Of course all of us need to understand the people to whom we minister, and all of us can benefit from small doses of such literature. But massive doses sooner or later dilute the gospel. Ever so subtly, we start to think that success more critically depends on thoughtful sociological analysis than on the gospel; Barna becomes more important than the Bible. We depend on plans, programs, vision statements—but somewhere along the way we have succumbed to the temptation to displace the foolishness of the cross with the wisdom of strategic planning. Again, I insist, my position is not a thinly veiled plea for obscurantism, for seat-of-the-pants ministry that plans nothing. Rather, I fear that the cross, without ever being disowned, is constantly in danger of being dismissed from the central place it must enjoy, by relatively peripheral insights that take on far too much weight. Whenever the periphery is in danger of displacing the center, we are not far removed from idolatry.

The Outreach of the Cross (1:26–31)

Although Paul has been sketching in how the message of the cross divides the human race, in large part he has focused on those who reject that message. Now he turns exclusively to those who accept it—and he finds that who they are supports his vision of what the message of the cross is about. By and large, he insists, the people who have accepted this message are not the wise, the glamorous, the gifted, the saintly. No—they are the nobodies.

Paul makes his point, offers a theological justification for it, and then ends with a Christian vision of boasting.

Paul's Point (1:26)

"Brothers," Paul addresses his fellow Christians, "think of what you were when you were called. Not many of you were wise by human standards; not many were influential; not many were of noble birth." At this point, Paul is dealing at the empirical level: these are the observable facts, and he wants the Corinthians to recognize them. When he tells them to consider what they were when they were "called," he means that he wants them to remember their station in life when they were converted.

And what were they? Not many were "wise," "influential," or "of noble birth" (1:26). Almost certainly Paul is adapting the language of Jeremiah 9:23–24, which he actually cites a few verses later (in 1 Cor. 1:31). In Jeremiah 9 the prophet quotes God as saying:

> "Let not the *wise man* boast of his wisdom
>   or the *strong man* boast of his strength
>   or the *rich man* boast of his riches,
> but let him who boasts boast about this:
>   that he understands and knows me,
>   that I am the LORD, who exercises kindness,
>   justice and righteousness on earth,
>   for in these I delight,"
> declares the LORD. [emphasis added]

Like Jeremiah, Paul speaks of the "wise." Jeremiah's "strong man" becomes, for Paul, the "influential"—that is, the strength in view is not the strength of the weight-lifter but the strength of the opinion-maker, the person with clout. The "rich man" becomes the person "of noble birth," since in preindustrial days the overwhelming majority of the wealthy sprang from the upper classes.

Paul recognizes, of course, that these categories have no eternal significance. He is talking about those who are wise "by human standards"—and implicitly about those who are influential or well born "by human standards." The particular expression he uses[3] suggests that he is strongly putting down those "human standards"; they are the standards of this world, this fallen world, over against those of God. Nevertheless, they are

---

3. Greek, *kata sarka* , lit., "according to the flesh."

the standards that most of society highly esteems. Paul reminds the Corinthian believers that "not many" of them met those standards.

Before we pursue Paul's argument any further, it is worth pausing to remember that some opponents of Christianity have sometimes tried to turn Paul's words against the gospel. They say that only the ignorant and the foolish become Christians. For example, in the second century the critic Celsus sneered at Christians in these terms:

> Their injunctions are like this. "Let no one educated, no one wise, no one sensible draw near. For these abilities are thought by us to be evils. But as for anyone ignorant, anyone stupid, anyone uneducated, anyone who is a child, let him come boldly." By the fact that they themselves admit that these people are worthy of their God, they show that they want and are able to convince only the foolish, dishonourable and stupid, and only slaves, women, and children. [Contra Celsum 3.44]

Along analogous lines, not a few contemporary intellectuals work very hard at conveying the impression that all Christians are fools or knaves or both. And on first reading, Paul might almost be taken to support this criticism.

More careful reading shows that Paul's point is rather different. In the first place, Paul repeatedly says "not many," not "not any." In the days of the great evangelist George Whitefield, the Countess of Huntingdon used to say that she was saved by an *m*: God's word declares "not *m*any noble," not "not any noble." Besides, it has been repeatedly shown that first-century Christianity was astonishingly heterogeneous. It was the only society in the empire that brought together slave and free, Jew and Gentile, rich and poor, male and female. If there were many poor, ill-educated people, many slaves and illiterates, there were also people like Crispus, Gaius, Philemon, Erastus—not to mention minds like Paul's.

So what then is Paul saying in this verse? His point, surely, is that being wise or influential or well born cannot possibly be a criterion of being a Christian or of being spiritual. If many in the Corinthian congregation were drawn from segments of society that were not highly regarded "by human standards," then no one could argue that the church was basically a high-class operation with a few exceptions to prove how open-minded it was. Rather, it was a low-class operation with a few sophisticated exceptions to prove that the "wise" and the "influential" and those "of noble birth" are not necessarily excluded.

God's grace can reach anyone. But being well regarded in the surrounding pagan society is in no sense an advantage. If anyone approaches God on the basis of some putative wisdom or "pull" or wealth, he or she is necessarily excluded. If God accepted people on such grounds, he would compromise himself. He would be the worst kind of snob, the kind that is impressed by entirely superficial advantages—like a panting, third-rate social climber in a pinstripe suit, desperate to be approved and eager to fawn all over anyone who speaks with a posh accent. Paul insists that such a vision of God is utter nonsense. God is not impressed by the public philosophies, political clout, and extravagant wealth that the world so greatly admires. And the Corinthian believers should have recognized the point and disavowed such pagan allegiances themselves. After all, the commonness of their own predominant backgrounds should have alerted them to the kind of people God frequently pursues.

This is a point that our generation cannot afford to ignore. Why is it that we constantly parade Christian athletes, media personalities, and pop singers? Why should we think that their opinions or their experiences of grace are of any more significance than those of any other believer? When we tell outsiders about people in our church, do we instantly think of the despised and the lowly who have become Christians, or do we love to impress people with the importance of the men and women who have become Christians? Modern Western evangelicalism is deeply infected with the virus of triumphalism, and the resulting illness destroys humility, minimizes grace, and offers far too much homage to the money and influence and "wisdom" of our day.

Paul's Theological Justification (1:27–30)

The empirical evidence, then, is that the Corinthian congregation was made up of people from a wide range of backgrounds, but that most of them could not boast of any great cultural superiority. Is there a fundamental reason for this?

Paul insists there is. God himself "chose the foolish things of the world to shame the wise; God chose the weak things of the world to shame the strong. He chose the lowly things of this world and the despised things—and the things that are not [today we would probably refer to 'the nobodies']—to nullify the things that are" (1:27–28). Paul presupposes that people will not come to Christ unless he chooses them. So if there are many "nobodies" who come to Christ, it can only mean that Christ has chosen them. The fundamental reason why there are not more big shots in the Christian church ("big shots" as measured "by human standards," 1:26) is that God has preferentially chosen the nobodies.

God has chosen the foolish things, Paul insists, "to shame the wise." This does not mean that he makes them feel ashamed, but that he shames them, he disgraces them. In exactly the same way, God has chosen the nobodies "to nullify the things that are" (1:28). In other words, God delights to prick all the pretensions of this rebellious world. Where proud men and women parade their mighty intellects, God chooses the simple; where wealthy people assess each other on the basis of their respective holdings, God chooses the poor; where self-centered leaders lust for power, God chooses the nobodies. All "the things that are"—that is, the things that appear to have substance and are highly promoted in this fallen world—are "nullified." They are written off as having no eternal significance, since God does not attach his salvation to any of them. In fact, he goes out of his way to overturn their presumption: God chooses the nobodies.

God's ultimate reason for this choice is of utmost importance: it is "so that no one may boast before him" (1:29). Not only has he shamed and nullified the world by choosing so many people whom the world does not highly esteem, God has taken this step to shatter human boasting. God acts to redeem fallen men and women because he is gracious, and for no other reason. He does not owe anyone in the world forgiveness and eternal life. If he gave out these wonderful gifts on the basis of a formula worked out by the immigration departments of many countries—the more education, skills, sophistication, and wealth you have, the easier it is to get in—then many of those who come to know God by faith in Jesus Christ would have a legitimate ground for boasting. But God takes the action he does "so that no one may boast before him." "I am the LORD; that is my name! I will not give my glory to another or my praise to idols" (Isa. 42:8). "For my own sake, for my own sake, I do this. How can I let myself be defamed? I will not yield my glory to another" (Isa. 48:11). Again and again Paul has to warn the Corinthians against the dangers in their boasting (e.g., 1 Cor. 3:21; 2 Cor. 10–13). If one has any deep understanding of the gospel, one must say, with Paul, "Where, then, is boasting? It is excluded" (Rom. 3:27).

In short, the Corinthians themselves constitute unassailable proof that God's categories of wisdom and power are radically different from those of the world. The outreach of the cross as measured by the profile of the Corinthian congregation confirms the message of the cross: salvation is God's free gift, secured by the ignominious death of his own Son. This odious death is God's triumphant act, his most dazzling and powerful deed, the action by which he disgraces and trashes all human pretensions. God's salvation springs from God's grace, and it is received by those who trust him—not by the "beautiful people" or by the rich and powerful. The Corinthian believers should have understood these things simply by looking at who they were when God saved them.

But there is one kind of boasting permitted to Christians. Indeed, it is mandated of them.

A Christian Vision of Boasting (1:30–31)

Paul is not saying that Christians have nothing to boast about. Rather, he is saying that if they boast about the things the world boasts about, they are boasting about the wrong things.

That is true even in the passage from Jeremiah to which Paul has already alluded. There God not only prohibits the wise, the strong, and the rich from boasting of their assets, but he adds, "let him who boasts boast about this: that he understands and knows me, that I am the LORD, who exercises kindness, justice and righteousness on earth, for in these I delight" (Jer. 9:24). Of course, this does not give sanction to self-centered religious fanatics to run around and claim that all their opinions about everything are right because they know the Lord. The point of this solemn utterance is that human boasting is vile precisely because it elevates self to the pinnacle of importance—and sad to tell, it is as possible to do that in the religious field as in any other. This sort of boasting is done in order to puff ourselves up. It indicates that we are focusing on what is transient, of no eternal importance.

The only thing of transcendent importance to human beings is the knowledge of God. This knowledge does not belong to those who endlessly focus on themselves. Those who truly come to know God delight just to know him. He becomes their center. They think of him, delight in him, boast of him. They want to know more and more what kind of God he is. As they learn that he is the God "who exercises kindness, justice and righteousness on earth," naturally they want those same values to prevail—not because their egos are bound up with certain arbitrary notions of, say, "justice," but because their center is God and they take their cues from him and his character. They boast in him.

And now God's most dramatic act of "kindness, justice and righteousness" has occurred—in the death of his Son. By this act God has ensured that countless men and women will truly know him, and know the kind of God he is. "It is because of him that you are in Christ Jesus" (1:30), Paul tells the Corinthians. That is, it is because God chose them, as the previous verses make clear, that they have become Christians, that they are now "in Christ Jesus." They have been reconciled to God; they know him who is eternal; they have tasted the blessed relief of sins forgiven. Thus, Christ Jesus, the crucified and risen Christ Jesus, is himself God's plan, God's wisdom; he "has become for us wisdom from God" (1:30). This is not the wisdom of the world, which cannot make room for the cross. This wisdom from God is the cross; it is "Christ crucified" (1:23). Far from being vain and pompous and of no eternal importance, this "wisdom" effects eternal changes and brings men and women into a deep relationship with the living God.

In short, this "wisdom," this plan, means nothing less than "our righteousness, holiness and redemption."[4] Lest anyone be

---

4. Some versions follow the KJV: ". . . Christ Jesus, who of God is made unto us wisdom, and righteousness, and sanctification, and redemption"—suggesting that there are *four* things that Christ here becomes for us. But both the Greek and the logic make more sense in the NIV: Christ "has become for us wisdom from God"—and then that wisdom is "fleshed out" in biblical categories to distinguish it from the wisdom of the world. *This* wisdom means our righteousness, our holiness, and our redemption.

tempted to think that God's wisdom is nothing more than a souped-up version of the world's wisdom, Paul immediately unpacks it in traditional biblical terms. This "wisdom" secures our "righteousness" (a term that reflects our legal standing before God), our "holiness" (a properly religious term that reflects the exclusive sphere to which we now belong), and our "redemption" (a term drawn from the slave trade to reflect our newfound freedom from sin, corruption, and death).

Small wonder, then, that Paul ends by directly quoting Jeremiah. "Therefore, as it is written: 'Let him who boasts boast in the Lord'" (1 Cor. 1:31). We are as foolish as the Corinthians when we make much of what cannot endure, when we promote the values and plans and programs of a world that is passing away as if they bear any deep significance. So misguided a course eloquently betrays how little we know God. For the better we know God, the more we will want all of our existence to revolve around him, and we will see that the only goals and plans that really matter are those that are somehow tied to God himself, and to our eternity with him. Did not Jesus tell his followers to store up for themselves treasures in heaven (Matt. 6:19–21)?

So the message of the cross must shape our ministry (1:18–25); the outreach of the cross confirms that message and drives us back to what is fundamental (1:26–31). But there is one more element to bear in mind.

The Preacher of the Cross (2:1–5)

Paul's own example should have told the Corinthian Christians that they were pursuing a dangerous path, for in his preaching he had self-consciously distanced himself from the rhetorical pomp of his day. He writes, "When I came to you, brothers, I did not come with eloquence or superior wisdom [both 'eloquence' and 'superior wisdom' probably here refer to form rather than content] as I proclaimed to you the testimony about God" (2:1).

It has been persuasively argued that Paul is alluding to the sophists of his day. Many intellectual movements greatly prized rhetoric. Philosophers were as widely praised for their oratory as for their content. But the sophists brought these ideals to new heights. Following fairly rigid and somewhat artificial conventions, these public speakers were praised and followed (and gained paying students!) in proportion to their ability to declaim in public assembly, to choose a theme and expatiate on it with telling power, and to speak convincingly and movingly in legal, religious, business, and political contexts. They enjoyed such widespread influence in the Mediterranean world, not least in Corinth, that public speakers who either could not meet their standards, or who for any reason chose not to, were viewed as seriously inferior.

It is difficult for us at the end of the twentieth century to appreciate how influential this allegiance to rhetoric was. There is at least a little hint in the fact that Paul finds it necessary to deal with the matter again in 2 Corinthians (see 10:9–10; 11:5–6). It is worth remembering that rhetoric was a central subject in most Western universities until the beginning of this century. The rise of print, radio, and especially television has so elevated "cool" communication that fiery oratory now seems rather strange—either quaint or dangerous. Television newsreaders maintain perfect poise and calm voices whether they are describing famine in the Sahel, reporting an earthquake that wiped out two hundred thousand people in central China, or announcing who won a basketball game.

But rhetoric brings with it many dangers. Those who pursue eloquence and high-sounding insight with precious little content are often doing little more than preening their own feathers. Such oratory made Paul nervous. It affords far too many temptations to pride to be safe for anyone interested in preaching the gospel of the crucified Messiah.

So Paul made a choice. He "resolved" (2:2) to adopt a more restrictive course, even though he was cutting across the stream of cultural expectations. When the pressure to "contextualize" the gospel jeopardizes the message of the cross by inflating human egos, the cultural pressures must be ignored.

Two misinterpretations of Paul's commitment must be strenuously avoided. First, it would be entirely improper to infer that Paul was an incompetent speaker, a bad communicator. When Paul and Barnabas were in Lystra, where the sophists' standards of rhetoric held little sway, the pagans identified Paul with Hermes, the Greek god of communication (whose Roman name was

Mercury) because Paul was the chief speaker (Acts 14:12). Doubtless Paul displayed many communicative skills and worked to improve the clarity and potency of his presentation. In Thessalonica he earnestly "reasoned," "explained," and "proved" that the Messiah had to suffer and rise from the dead (Acts 17:2–3). What Paul avoided was artificial communication that won plaudits for the speaker but distracted from the message. Lazy preachers have no right to appeal to 1 Corinthians 2:1–5 to justify indolence in the study and careless delivery in the pulpit. These verses do not prohibit diligent preparation, passion, clear articulation, and persuasive presentation. Rather, they warn against any method that leads people to say, "What a marvelous preacher!" rather than, "What a marvelous Savior!"

Second, we would be entirely mistaken if we concluded on the basis of this passage that Paul was insensitive to cultural peculiarities among the diverse groups he evangelized, and therefore we need not bother with such niceties ourselves. In fact, Paul was astonishingly flexible. This point can be demonstrated by appealing to the Book of Acts and comparing, say, Paul's sermon in Pisidian Antioch in a Jewish synagogue (Acts 13:13–41) with his sermon in the Areopagus in Athens, in a decidedly pagan context (Acts 17:16–31). But the point can be made even more forcefully by appealing to Paul's own writings, not least 1 Corinthians. We shall return to this remarkable flexibility in the last chapter of this book, where we look more closely at some parts of 1 Corinthians 9. For the moment it is enough to insist that, however great Paul's flexibility and cultural sensitivity, they are not open-ended; he draws the line where he thinks the gospel might be jeopardized. And clearly he thinks the gospel is jeopardized by any kind of eloquence or rhetoric that does not reinforce the message of a crucified Messiah. Clever, witty, amusing, glittering discourse may be warmly applauded by the literati, but it does not easily square with the odium of the cross. So Paul will have none of it.

Neither would the early English Puritans. In an age when scholars often used the pulpit to display their great learning, the Puritans resolved to speak with simplicity and forcefulness calculated to do their hearers the most good. Their sermons were designed to benefit their hearers with the eternal gospel, not to

win applause from other learned preachers. When Thomas
Goodwin went up to Cambridge University in 1613, he desired to
emulate the best "witty" preachers, such as Dr. Senhouse of St.
John's College. But after his conversion, Goodwin adopted the
Puritan principle:

> I came to this resolved principle, that I would preach wholly and
> altogether sound and wholesome words, without affectation of
> wit and vanity of eloquence. . . . I . . . have continued in that pur-
> pose and practice these threescore years. I have preached what I
> thought was truly edifying, either for conversion, or bringing
> them up to eternal life.[5]

But I understood this point most clearly, I think, when I
heard of an Egyptian believer with extraordinary communication skills. Arabic is a language that operates on two levels.
There is a sort of street Arabic—or, more precisely, there are
several quite different street Arabics, depending on the region—
and a "high" or "literary" Arabic. The latter may be found not
only in good Arabic literature, but, in the hands of the skillful,
it may be found in oral address. This particular Egyptian Christian was a journalist, widely read as much for the music of his
prose as for the quality of his content. He felt called of God to
Christian ministry, abandoned journalism, and soon built up a
very large congregation. Many of those who attended his
church did so simply because they greatly enjoyed listening to
his orations.

But this preacher was troubled. He discovered that many people were far more interested in his Arabic than his Savior. After
much soul-searching, he switched to the more colloquial Arabic.
His reasoning was quite simple: his purpose was to convey the
message of the cross, and he had come to the conclusion that his
rhetoric was getting in the way. That man, surely, understood
Paul.

What gets in our way?

It would probably be invidious of me to try to make a list of
things that might get in the way in our culture, not least because

---

5. Thomas Goodwin, *Works*, ed. J. Miller (London: James Nichol, 1861), 2.1xivf.
Cited in J. I. Packer, *A Quest for Godliness: The Puritan Vision of the Christian Life*
(Wheaton: Crossway, 1990), 74.

they vary from region to region, but also because culture keeps changing. Instead, it will be a wiser and more enduring course to summarize the values Paul the preacher sets forth:

Proclaim the testimony about God. That is what Paul did: "I proclaimed to you the testimony[6] about God" (2:1). Earlier we saw that God was pleased to save those who believe "through the foolishness of what was preached" (1:21), the focus being on the content. Nevertheless, Paul writes of "the foolishness of what was preached," not "the foolishness of what was discussed or commented on or shared." So also here: the content of Paul's message is "the testimony about God" (that is, what God has done in Christ Jesus). But what Paul does with this message is proclaim it. He preaches it.

Granted that "preaching" or "proclaiming" in the Scriptures is not restricted to something done behind a wooden pulpit between 11:00 and 12:00 on Sunday mornings, it is nevertheless hard to avoid the strength of this emphasis on proclamation in the New Testament. The reason for the emphasis lies in the message itself. God has taken action, and the good news is announced, it is proclaimed. God is not negotiating; he is both announcing and confronting. Done properly, preaching is simply the re-presentation of God's gospel, God's good news, by which men and women come to know him. Thus preaching mediates God himself. Many preachers, afraid of being thought arrogant, avoid talking about preaching. They prefer to think of what they do as "sharing." In some limited contexts, doubtless there is nothing wrong with "sharing." But something important is lost if we never speak or think of preaching and proclamation. That is our job, our calling. It is not arrogant to re-present as forcefully as we can God's gospel; it is simply faithful stewardship. Further, if we focus on the powerful proclamation of the gospel, we shall be less likely to be seduced by siren calls to soften the sheer non-negotiability inherent in preaching.

Focus on Christ crucified. That is what Paul did: "For I resolved to know nothing while I was with you except Jesus Christ and him crucified" (2:2). This does not mean that this was a new

---

6. Some manuscripts read "the mystery of God" rather than [lit.] "the testimony about God." The difference is very slight in Greek and makes little difference to my argument here.

departure for Paul, still less that Paul was devoted to blissful ignorance of anything and everything other than the cross. No, what he means is that all he does and teaches is tied to the cross. He cannot long talk about Christian joy, or Christian ethics, or Christian fellowship, or the Christian doctrine of God, or anything else, without finally tying it to the cross. Paul is gospel-centered; he is cross-centered.

That is more than a creedal commitment; it sets out Paul's priorities, his lifestyle, and, in this context, his style of ministry. If he really holds that God has supremely disclosed himself in the cross and that to follow the crucified and risen Savior means dying daily, then it is preposterous to adopt a style of ministry that is triumphalistic, designed to impress, calculated to win applause. It is precisely because Paul resolves "to know nothing . . . except Jesus Christ and him crucified" that he can formulate his policy on rhetoric.

What then does it mean today to resolve "to know nothing . . . except Jesus Christ and him crucified"? More narrowly, what elements in our ministries need overhauling when judged by this standard? For this commitment must not only shape our message but our style.

We have become so performance-oriented that it is hard to see how compromised we are. Consider one small example. In many of our churches, prayers in morning services now function, in large measure, as the time to change the set in the sanctuary. The people of the congregation bow their heads and close their eyes, and when they look up a minute later, why, the singers are in place, or the drama group is ready to perform. It is all so smooth. It is also profane. Nominally we are in prayer together addressing the King of heaven, the sovereign Lord. In reality, some of us are doing that while others are rushing on tiptoes around the "stage" and others, with their eyes closed, are busy wondering what new and happy configuration will confront them when it is time to take a peek.

Has the smoothness of the performance become more important to us than the fear of the Lord? Has polish, one of the modern equivalents of ancient rhetoric, displaced substance? Have professional competence and smooth showmanship become more valuable than sober reckoning over what it means to focus on Christ crucified?

Do not fear weakness, illness, or a sense of being overwhelmed. The truth of the matter is that such experiences are often the occasions when God most greatly displays his power. As long as people are impressed by your powerful personality and impressive gifts, there is very little room for you to impress them with a crucified Savior. "I came to you," Paul confesses, "in weakness and fear, and with much trembling" (2:3)—so much so that he needed special encouragement from God himself (Acts 18:9–10). But Paul knew that God's strength is most greatly displayed in connection with our weakness (2 Cor. 12:1–10). Although he suffered fears, illness, weakness, and a tremendous sense of being overwhelmed by the enormity of the task, he did not fear the fear; his weakness was not compounded by focusing on his weakness. Far from it! He could write, "That is why, for Christ's sake, I delight in weaknesses, in insults, in hardships, in persecutions, in difficulties. For when I am weak, then I am strong" (2 Cor. 12:10). That is the testimony of a man who has learned to minister under the cross.

Strenuously avoid manipulating people. "My message and my preaching were not with wise and persuasive words" (2:4), Paul writes. He does not mean that there is no sense in which he sets out to be persuasive. Elsewhere he testifies, "Since, then, we know what it is to fear the Lord, we try to persuade men" (2 Cor. 5:11). But he avoids persuasion that is manipulative; he eschews preaching that cajoles or moves people by its eloquence but does not faithfully present the gospel. It is the truth and power of the gospel that must change people's lives, not the glamour of our oratory or the emotional power of our stories.

Some years ago I was speaking at a large youth convention in Australia. Never was I more impressed with the leader and organizer of these meetings than when he addressed the three or four hundred site and group leaders and quietly told them to avoid manipulation. Ensure that the young people get enough sleep, he said. We do not want decisions just because they are so tired their stamina is worn down. Do not put these people into emotional corners that compel decisions; such decisions are seldom worth anything. Do not shame them or embarrass them in front of peers. Deal straightforwardly with the gospel.

This leader was simply following the advice of Paul. He was more interested in the integrity of his presentation, which he could not divorce from the integrity of the gospel itself, than with the pressure for impressive statistics.

Recognize that a cross-centered ministry is characterized by the Spirit's power and is vindicated in transformed lives. Paul's message was attended "with a demonstration of the Spirit's power, so that [the] faith [of his converts] might not rest on men's wisdom, but on God's power" (2:4–5).

That is what we need: unction, the anointing of the Spirit, the demonstration of the Spirit's power. Where that power is present, people cannot help but know it, and the faith of those who turn to Christ is safely anchored in God himself. Where that power is absent, nothing can repair the loss, and the faith of new converts is likely to be attached, in part, to the wrong things.

But Paul will say more about the Spirit in the following verses.

Concluding Reflections

The message of the cross smashes the great idolatries of the ecclesiastical world: our endless self-promotion, our love of mere professionalism, our addiction to well-defined methods. Doubtless in some circumstances it might be wrong to criticize any one of these tendencies. Yet taken together they weave a pattern of ministry that is so far removed from the message of the cross, the demonstrable outreach of the cross, and this New Testament description of the preacher of the cross, that we must confess in shame that we have turned to idols and must repent of our sin.

Biblical preaching emphasizes the gospel and constantly elevates Christ crucified. But it also recognizes that the cross is not only our creed, it is the standard of our ministry.

Questions for Review and Reflection

1. Why do human beings find the cross of Jesus Christ so unpalatable?
2. Explain what Paul means when he speaks of "the foolishness of God."
3. Why does God so often save "nobodies"? What significance does your answer have for you personally?
4. What does it mean to "boast in the Lord"? Do you boast that way?
5. Summarize Paul's view of what preaching should be, according to this passage.

2

The Cross and the Holy Spirit
1 Corinthians 2:6–16

[6]We do, however, speak a message of wisdom among the mature, but not the wisdom of this age or of the rulers of this age, who are coming to nothing. [7]No, we speak of God's secret wisdom, a wisdom that has been hidden and that God destined for our glory before time began. [8]None of the rulers of this age understood it, for if they had, they would not have crucified the Lord of glory. [9]However, as it is written:

> "No eye has seen,
> no ear has heard,
> no mind has conceived
> what God has prepared for those who love
>   him"—

[10]but God has revealed it to us by his Spirit. The Spirit searches all things, even the deep things of God. [11]For who among men knows the thoughts of a man except the man's spirit within him? In the

same way no one knows the thoughts of God except the Spirit of God. [12]We have not received the spirit of the world but the Spirit who is from God, that we may understand what God has freely given us.

[13]This is what we speak, not in words taught us by human wisdom but in words taught by the Spirit, expressing spiritual truths in spiritual words. [14]The man without the Spirit does not accept the things that come from the Spirit of God, for they are foolishness to him, and he cannot understand them, because they are spiritually discerned. [15]The spiritual man makes judgments about all things, but he himself is not subject to any man's judgment:

[16]"For who has known the mind of the Lord that he may instruct him?" But we have the mind of Christ.

It is more than a little ironic that a passage that should teach us to be humble has been used by some people to justify an astonishing measure of arrogance. These people voice their opinions as to what God is like and what God is doing, and if you challenge them at any point they may reply in the words of Paul in verse 12: "We have not received the spirit of the world but the Spirit who is from God, that we may understand what God has freely given us." More than once I have been informed that, by contrast, I am one of the people Paul describes in verse 14: "The man without the Spirit does not accept the things that come from the Spirit of God, for they are foolishness to him, and he cannot understand them, because they are spiritually discerned." In other words, if you agree with such people, you are spiritual; if you disagree, you are not. Press them a little harder, and ask how they know their interpretation is correct and what checks they accept on their own authority, and they may reply, with supreme confidence, in the words of verse 15: "The spiritual man makes judgments about all things, but he himself is not subject to any man's judgment." In the worst cases, this leads to flagrant authoritarianism—utterly self-focused leaders who are accountable to no one but themselves.

Almost by way of reaction, other people have argued that this passage says nothing about the Spirit helping people to understand the truth, but only about the Spirit helping people to apply the truth to themselves. If biblical interpretation is held hostage to some sort of mystical experience of the Spirit, they say, and taken out of the realm of words, history, grammar, and exegesis, then there is no logical stopping place. At the end of the day we are locked into subjectivism, each opinion claiming to be taught by the Spirit. Biblical interpretation has to be out there in the marketplace of ideas, and atheistic Bible interpreters can be just as right, just as often, as faithful, believing interpreters—it's just that apart from the Spirit they are unable to apply the text that they rightly interpret to themselves. Of course, this sounds like a wonderful defense of the objectivity of truth. But one might be excused for thinking that this is not an obvious reading of verses 12–16.

In fact, from the Reformation on, these verses have been used primarily to justify quite a different proposition. Here the point has been that those "without the Spirit" (v. 14) are so dead that it is folly to think that arguments can bring them to faith. The things of the Spirit are simply "foolishness" to such people, who "cannot understand them, because they are spiritually discerned." In other words, the Holy Spirit himself must do an antecedent work in our hearts and minds if we are going to believe. Without his help, gospel truths will always seem alien to us.

That is much closer to what this passage is about, but even so it is important to set the chapter in its context. If we are to make sense of this passage and discover how the cross of Christ remains a controlling theme, we must do two things.

First, we must steadfastly grasp that this passage is a continuation of the argument begun in 1:18. As we have seen, the last half of chapter 1 exalts "the message of the cross" (1:18) over against the "wisdom" of the world. When he talks about his own priorities as a preacher (2:1–5), Paul is still talking about the message of the cross. His "message" and his "preaching" (2:4) have as their content not "wise and persuasive words" but "Jesus Christ and him crucified" (2:2). So when Paul now goes on to insist that his message is in one sense "a message of wisdom" after all (2:6), we are not to think that Paul has gravitated to some new message. Far from it: he is still talking about what it meant when "the rulers of this age . . . crucified the Lord of glory" (2:8). In other words, Paul has not launched into a new topic, a fresh discussion of esoteric wisdom. He is still focused on the message of the cross—and we shall fail to understand this chapter unless we bear that fact in mind.

Second, we must observe that the argument in these verses is largely set up in terms of three controlling contrasts. These three contrasts overlap a little, and they must be rightly understood.

First Contrast: Those Who Receive God's Wisdom and Those Who Do Not (2:6–10a)

Paul has already shown (in 1:18–25) that the message of the crucified Messiah, judged by the world to be just so much nonsense, is in fact the most momentous display of God's wisdom. For some it is a message of weakness and foolishness, but for those who believe, Christ is both "the power of God and the wisdom of God" (1:24). At this point Paul wants to unpack a little more just what it is in this wisdom that makes it impossible for people to recognize it, the more so if they themselves have ostensibly been pursuing God's wisdom.

So Paul begins to set up the contrast. He has just finished explaining his own resolution to avoid manipulative rhetoric, mere eloquence, but he does not want for a moment to risk giving the impression that the message of the cross is "foolish" in every sense: "We do, however, speak a message of wisdom among the mature, but not the wisdom of this age or of the rulers of this age, who are coming to nothing" (2:6). The one word in this verse that has precipitated endless discussion is the word *mature*, sometimes rendered "perfect." Very often the word is connected with a subset of all true believers, namely, the "mature" believers. In other words, taken in this way it implicitly introduces a distinction in the fellowship of Christians: there are mature believers, and there are immature believers—a point that Paul himself makes at the beginning of chapter 3, as we shall see.

But such an interpretation really does not fit here. The *mature* in this context really must refer to all Christians, who cherish the message of the cross, over against the world that rejects the message of the cross. The question then becomes, Why does Paul choose this word, the word *mature*, to describe all Christians in this context? Could he not have guessed that it would lead to all kinds of misinterpretation?

Almost certainly Paul chose this word because the Corinthians themselves loved it—and loved to apply it to themselves. They thought of themselves as mature, and, without suggesting that Paul was not a Christian, they thought of Paul and his message as immature. In the next chapter Paul will find it necessary to tell them that, within the Christian camp, they are the ones who are immature (3:1–4). But before he gets there, he must challenge their fundamental categories. All Christians are "mature" in the sense that they have come to terms with the message of the cross, while all others, by definition, have not. The message of Christ crucified is the only fundamental dividing line in the human race.

Paul's point is then reasonably clear. Just as our "message of wisdom" is "not the wisdom of this age" (2:6), so those who accept God's message of wisdom do not belong to this age. In fact, "the wisdom of this age," even if the rulers of this age espouse it, remains without eternal value. The rulers themselves "are coming to nothing" (2:6). Why then should Christians be infatuated with paper heroes who win the passing applause of a dying world, but who from an eternal perspective are without significance? They remind the reader of those the psalmist describes: not only will the wicked perish, but "the way of the wicked will perish" (Ps. 1:6).

The "rulers of this age" is not here a reference to demons or even restrictively to political leaders, but rather to those who rule the outlook and values of any age—the "wise man," the "scholar," and the "philosopher" of 1:20 and the "wise," the "influential," and those "of noble birth" of 1:26. They are the best the world can advance, yet they oppose the message of the cross. Why then should we side with them as to what is important?

Their wisdom is without ultimate value. It is not what we proclaim. "No," Paul writes, accenting the difference between the "rulers" and what Christians cherish, "we speak of God's secret wisdom, a wisdom that has been hidden and that God destined for our glory before time began" (2:7, emphasis added). This "wisdom," the wisdom of the cross, is characterized by three things.

First, it is, literally, "wisdom in a mystery," what the New International Version calls "God's secret wisdom" (2:7). It is wisdom "that has been hidden" for a long time, but that has now been revealed. That is the dominant meaning of mystery in the New Testament (often rendered "secret" or "secret things" in the NIV). That means that Paul thinks of the message of the cross as something that had been hidden in the past, but that has now been revealed.

We need to think rather carefully about this. The New Testament writers are constantly saying that the coming of Jesus Christ and the good news he brings have been prophesied in the ancient Scriptures. Here and in many other places, Paul (and some other New Testament writers too, for that matter) argues that the coming of Jesus Christ and the good news he brings have been hidden in the past but are now revealed. How can exactly the same gospel be said, on the one hand, to have been prophesied and now fulfilled, and on the other, to have been hidden but now revealed?

The question is not an easy one and is tied to some of the most disputed matters in the history of the church. I cannot probe these things here. But I do note that in one remarkable passage Paul dares to bring both of these themes together. At the end of Romans, he writes,

> Now to him who is able to establish you by my gospel and the proclamation of Jesus Christ, according to the *revelation of the mystery hidden for long ages past, but now revealed and made known through the prophetic writings* by the command of the eternal God, so that all nations might believe and obey him—to the only wise God be glory forever through Jesus Christ! Amen. [Rom. 16:25–27, emphasis added]

This is astonishing. At one and the same time, Paul says that the gospel has been "hidden for long ages past," yet now that it has been revealed and made known this act of disclosure is through the prophetic writings! So is it hidden or not?[1] If it has been hidden, how can it be made known through the Scriptures? If it is

---

1. It is possible to translate the verse slightly differently, but the substance of the tension I have described is not alleviated.

now made known through the Scriptures, how can one reasonably say that it has been hidden, when the Old Testament Scriptures have been around for a long time?

Paul's point, I think, is that believing the Old Testament Scriptures are true is not enough. After all, until he became a Christian, Paul himself passionately believed in what we would today call the Old Testament—but that did not ensure that he found there the message of the crucified Messiah. It was not until he met the resurrected Jesus on the Damascus road that he was forced to reexamine the entire structure of his beliefs. And then he read the Old Testament with new eyes. I briefly traced some of that thought in the first chapter of this book.

The point is that however much the Old Testament points to Jesus, much of this prophecy is in veiled terms—in types and shadows and structures of thought. The sacrificial system prepares the way for the supreme sacrifice; the office of high priest anticipates the supreme intermediary between God and sinful human beings, the man Christ Jesus; the passover displays God's wrath and provides a picture of the ultimate passover lamb whose blood averts that wrath; the announcement of a new covenant (Jer. 31) and a new priesthood (Ps. 110) pronounce the obsolescence in principle of the old covenant and priesthood. Hypothetically, if there had been some perfect people around to observe what was going on, people with an unblemished heart for God, they might well have observed the patterns and understood the plan. But the world has been peopled with sinners since the fall, and the Old Testament Scriptures God gave were often in some measure misunderstood. That there was human fault in this misunderstanding is presupposed by Jesus himself when he berates his followers: "How foolish you are, and how slow of heart to believe all that the prophets have spoken! Did not the Christ have to suffer these things and then enter his glory?" (Luke 24:25–26). Yet at the same time, these matters *had* to be veiled. If the prophecies about Jesus had all been crystal clear and absolutely specific and univocal, one could not imagine how the Sanhedrin and Pontius Pilate and Herod could have so radically misunderstood what they were doing. True, they should have understood anyway. But, Paul says, empirically none of them did: "None of the rulers of this age understood it, for if they had, they would not have crucified the Lord of glory" (2:8). Thus, it was God's wise plan to have wicked human beings effect his own good purposes of redemption; it was his matchless grace and wisdom that provided revelation clear enough to be understood after the events to which it pointed had occurred, but veiled enough that rebellious sinners would in some measure misinterpret it and put it together in wrong ways.

So the "message of wisdom," the message of the cross that we proclaim, is "God's secret wisdom," a wisdom that was in large measure hidden for long ages until the Messiah was crucified.

Second, this wisdom has always been God's plan, and he destined it "for our glory before time began" (2:7). Paul would not want any of his readers to think that, just because it has in some measure been hidden in the past, its present unveiling therefore marks it as brand new, some fresh departure in the mind of God. Far from it. In God's mind it stretches back "before time began." And it was God himself who decided to bring it to full disclosure now; in short, he "destined [it] for our glory."

This is a wonderful thought, and one to which other New Testament writers allude. Peter said that it was revealed to Old Testament Scripture writers "that they were not serving themselves but you, when they spoke of the things that have now been told you by those who have preached the gospel" (1 Pet. 1:12). Jesus Christ "was chosen before the creation of the world, but was revealed in these last times for your sake" (1 Pet. 1:20). At one level, even some of the moral lessons derivable from the sad accounts of human failure and defection under the old covenant are for our good: "These things happened to them as examples and were written down as warnings for us, on whom the fulfillment of the ages has come" (1 Cor. 10:11). The great heroes of faith under the old covenant did not themselves receive what had been promised; "God had planned something better for us so that only together with us would they be made perfect" (Heb. 11:40).

Implicitly, of course, this means it is the most astonishing folly for the Corinthians to adopt the positions espoused by the esteemed authorities of a culture that does not know God. God has purposed to bring his plan of redemption to fruition in the lives of all believers who live this side of the cross. Why then should they depreciate this matchless heritage from God

Almighty by becoming infatuated with the faddish fancies of the cross-denying opinion-makers who belong to an age that is passing away? It is all so ironic and tragic.

In fact, the irony begins with Jesus' brutal death. The authorities who crucified Jesus were in fact, quite unwittingly, carrying out God's purposes. As the praying Christians put it in Acts 4, "indeed Herod and Pontius Pilate met together with the Gentiles and the people of Israel in this city to conspire against your holy servant Jesus, whom you anointed. They did what your power and will had decided beforehand should happen" (Acts 4:27–28). They thought they were doing away with a messianic pretender; in fact, they were illegally and immorally executing "the Lord of glory." They thought they were so wise, so politically astute; in fact, by their folly they brought to pass, in God's perfect providence, his own wise plan—the very plan that they dismissed as foolishness. Amazing grace: in God's wise purposes, they killed the Lord of life.

Paul concludes his point by citing Scripture, apparently an amalgam from Isaiah 64:4 and 65:17 in the Greek Old Testament he was using. "No eye has seen, no ear has heard, no mind has conceived what God has prepared for those who love him" (2:9). Of course not, since God's wise plan was at that point still "secret," still "in a mystery," largely hidden. "But"[2] now "God has revealed it to us" (2:10).

So although these words are often quoted at funerals to refer to what glories await the believer after death (which is surely a good thought), Paul uses these words to refer to what has been hidden in the past but is now revealed to believers.

Again, then, we discover how wretchedly foolish it is to honor with our allegiance the siren opinion-makers of our day, if they have no real understanding of the cross. To us has been given the

---

2. Some manuscripts read "For" instead of "But" at the beginning of verse 10. In that case the flow of thought would be a bit different. Verse 10a would then ground the truth that God has prepared these things for those who love him—for God has revealed these things to us by his Spirit. But the general thought is not changed: the things that have not been perceived by human eye, ear, or mind have now been revealed to us. Perhaps I should add that the syntax of the quotation in verse 9 is rather difficult. Translated rather pedantically, it probably runs like this: "What no eye has seen, what no ear has heard, what no mind has conceived, [is] what God has prepared for those who love him."

fantastic privilege of benefiting from God's immeasurably wise plan of redemption. Shall we sell this awesome heritage for a mess of faddish pottage?

There is no deep and stable spirituality that does not acknowledge what an utterly profound privilege it is to know God and be reconciled to him by the crucified Messiah.

But there is a third element that characterizes the wisdom of God. Paul barely refers to it, and then it takes over in his presentation and becomes the locus of the second contrast. It is this: Even though God has now so definitively brought his all-wise plan to fruition in the gospel of the crucified Messiah, people still do not believe. They still do not see that his plan is wise. If we the "mature" have come to grasp it, it is because "God has revealed it to us by his Spirit" (2:10).

In other words, there has not only been an objective, public act of divine self-disclosure in the crucifixion of God's own Son, but there must also be a private work of God, by his Spirit, in the mind and heart of the individual. That is what distinguishes the believer from the unbeliever, the "mature" from the people of this age and the rulers of this age. If we "see" the truth of the gospel, therefore, it has nothing to do with our brilliance or insight; it has to do with the Spirit of God. If we should express unqualified gratitude to God for the gift of his Son, we should express no less gratitude to God for the gift of the Spirit who enables us to grasp the gospel of his Son.

And that brings us to the second contrast.

Second Contrast: The Spirit of God and the Spirit of the World (2:10b–13)

We have learned that those who receive God's wisdom, the message of the cross, are distinguished from "this age" by the Spirit of God, who reveals this wisdom to them. But why should this sort of "outside" help be needed? "Knowledge is knowledge," someone might say. "If God has disclosed himself in real events in real history, why should he still be so inaccessible to some people? Despite all they say, aren't Christians making an appeal to an esoteric, non-testable kind of knowledge that not everyone can enjoy?"

But note how the question has been put. It has been cast exclusively in terms of empirical knowledge—like the kind of knowledge that is based on repeatable experiments in a chemistry laboratory. But all of us are intuitively aware of other dimensions of "knowledge." For instance, our observation of a concrete historical event at which we were present, or our knowledge of people, or of a specific person, is tied to personal experience of a sort that is not strictly repeatable. How much more difficult is it to understand exactly what is meant by "knowing" God—a Being on a different order from the horizontal relationships that ordinarily occupy us?

Add one more factor: the problem is not only that God is much greater than we are, but that we are so rebellious that we distort much of the information about himself that he has graciously provided. If we are deeply infected with "the spirit of the world" (v. 12), if "human wisdom" (v. 13) is what we normally lean on, we must recognize, shamefacedly, that in 1 Corinthians 1–2 Paul does not give us a very high estimate of such "advantages."

Paul's point, then, is that the possibility of knowing God and of understanding his ways does not belong to any human being as an essential component of his or her being. The distance is too great; our self-centeredness is too deep. And nothing in "the wisdom of this age" (v. 6) can help us.

> A wisdom proper to this age is . . . one that arises out of and is marked by rebellion against God; it represents (however splendid and spiritual—or scientific—it may appear) the creature's attempt to secure his position over against the Creator; in a word it is (as far as men are concerned) man-centred.[3]

What is required, then, is revelation. The agent who brings such revelation to us is the Spirit of God.

Among "knowing" beings—humans, angels, God—there are high barriers that keep one knowing being from understanding fully what another knowing being is thinking about. No matter how well I know you, I will never know all your thoughts; no matter how well you know me, you will never know all of mine. How

---

3. C. K. Barrett, *A Commentary on the First Epistle to the Corinthians* (New York: Harper & Row, 1968), 70.

much less shall we understand the thoughts of the angel Gabriel when, say, he spoke to Mary (Luke 1:26–38). However, the one "knowing being" who knows all thoughts, even the thoughts of God, is God himself. Or, to put it another way, "The Spirit searches all things, even the deep things of God" (2:10b).

The word *spirit*, of course, is flexible in the Bible. It can be used to refer to the "interior" of a human being, the "inmost part"—almost equivalent to *mind*. Thus when Paul asks, "For who among men knows the thoughts of a man except the man's spirit within him?" (2:11), he means that the thoughts of an individual human being are in large measure masked to all other human beings. Only the one person really knows what that one person is thinking. Of course, this is a human limitation: "Who among men knows the thoughts" of another? God faces no such limitations as he searches our thoughts; we certainly face that limitation when we try to discern one another's thoughts, let alone his. Using the same language of "spirit," Paul drives his point home: "In the same way no one knows the thoughts of God except the Spirit of God" (v. 11). That means that if we are to understand God, to think his thoughts after him, truly to "know" him, we are going to have to receive the Spirit of God. We simply cannot find him by ourselves.

But we Christians have received the Spirit of God; that is what constitutes us Christians. "We have not received the spirit of the world but the Spirit who is from God" (2:12), and the purpose of this gift is "that we may understand what God has freely given us" (2:12). Now we see the two primary dimensions of revelation very clearly. The first is in the public arena. The words "what God has freely given us" refer to the cross of the Messiah and all that he has achieved for us. These things come to us out of God's matchless grace; he "has freely given" his people these gifts. The cross achieves the redemption of the people of God; it also displays God's unfathomable wisdom, bringing to open display a plan that had mercifully been "hidden" in ages past. But the sad fact is that even so we would not have understood "what God has freely given us." Such understanding is dependent on a second dimension of revelation, one that takes place within the individual. Without it, no one would ever have understood what God had revealed of himself and of his wisdom in the public arena.

Our obtuseness, our deep self-centeredness, our love of pomp and power and prestige, simply would not have allowed us to understand the cross or our need of it. In short, our very lostness demanded the work of the Spirit of God, to the end that we might "understand what God has freely given us" (2:12).

What a great God we have! Not only does he redeem us through the ignominious crucifixion of his much-loved Son, but he sends us his Spirit to enable us to understand what he has done. So obtuse and blind are we that we would not have begun to grasp "what God has freely given us" unless God had taken this additional step.

But it is this same Spirit who has prompted Paul to preach the message the way he has. This message, writes Paul, "is what we speak, not in words taught us by human wisdom but in words taught by the Spirit, expressing spiritual truths in spiritual words" (2:13). The Greek of this last clause is difficult,[4] but the New International Version has probably got it right: "expressing spiritual truths in spiritual words." But what does this mean? It surely means something like this: In his ministry, Paul, prompted by the Spirit, found himself explaining spiritual things (the message of the cross, brought home to people by the Spirit, v. 12) in spiritual words—that is, in words appropriate to the nature of the

---

4. Greek, *all en didaktois pneumatos, pneumatikois pneumatika sugkrinontes*. The principal three options are: (1) NIV: "expressing spiritual truths in spiritual words"; (2) NIV margin: "interpreting spiritual truths to spiritual men"; (3) KJV: "comparing spiritual things with spiritual." The determining interpretative points are two: (a) The meaning of *sugkrinontes*. This verb is found only three times in the New Testament, both also in Paul (2 Cor. 10:12, used twice), where the context suggests the verb means "to compare." Many interpreters find that sufficient reason for siding with the KJV, the third option. They insist that the verb never has the sense of "to explain" or "to interpret," either in classical Greek or, of course, in the two other occurrences of the verb in the New Testament. True enough. But two out of three is not an overwhelming statistical advantage. More importantly, this verb regularly means "to explain" or "to interpret" in the Septuagint, representing the sort of Greek translation of the Old Testament from which Paul quarried not a little of his religious vocabulary. And other things being equal, that is the meaning that makes the most sense here. (b) The meaning of *pneumatikois* in the last clause. Does it refer to the "words taught by the Spirit" (taking the word as neuter) or to "spiritual people" (taking the word as masculine)? If the latter, perhaps anticipating the argument in verse 14, then the second meaning (NIV margin) is correct. In fact, the syntax strongly favors the first meaning; *pneumatikois* refers to *didaktois pneumatos*, justifying the first reading (NIV). If *pneumatikois* had referred to people, one would have expected an article.

message. In other words, Paul insists it is the Holy Spirit himself who has taught him to avoid the "wisdom of word" that empties the cross of its power (1:17) and who has led him to eschew the kind of fancy, rhetorical preaching characterized by "wise and persuasive words" (2:1–5).

Above all, then, Paul focuses on the message of the cross. The spirit of the world cannot make sense of it; the Spirit of God enables those who have this Spirit to understand it. That same Spirit prompts the spiritually-minded, like Paul, to preach it and teach it in appropriate ways. They will strenuously avoid all ostentatious display; they will abandon all cheap manipulation; they will be happy to embrace the scandal of the cross, for the cross is what has redeemed them. They will be wary of "gospel" preaching that talks much about God meeting our needs and enabling us to feel fulfilled, if it is not squarely anchored in the message of the cross. They will want to use plain, clear, forceful, truthful, frank, compassionate, compelling, cross-centered speech—"spiritual" language that is appropriate to the spiritual message they are bearing. For they recognize that the Spirit of God who has opened their eyes to embrace the cross has also taught them to proclaim "Christ crucified" in a way that conforms with the humbling immensity of the message.

Third Contrast: The "Natural" Person and the "Spiritual" Person (2:14–16)

One might be forgiven for thinking that Paul has dealt with these fundamental contrasts long enough. He has contrasted those who receive God's wisdom with those who do not (2:6–10a); he has contrasted the Spirit of God with the spirit of the world (2:10b–13). Why this further step? Might it not be a bit redundant?

But Paul wants to make sure that his readers fully grasp their utter dependence on the Holy Spirit, for nothing else will so quickly humble their endless pretensions to greatness and all the divisiveness, self-centeredness, and lovelessness that follow hard on the heels of such puffery. That is why the apostle takes this further step.

What Paul does, then, is contrast "the man without the Spirit" (v. 14; some translations render this "the natural man") with "the spiritual man" (v. 15). By the time he has finished with this contrast he will have made it very clear why we must have the Holy Spirit if we are to make sense of the gospel at all. Paul says two things about those who do not have the Spirit, about these "natural" people.

First, he insists that they do not "accept the things that come from the Spirit of God" for a very simple reason: such things "are foolishness" to them. At this point Paul is not insisting that human beings without the Spirit are unable to grasp spiritual things (though that is exactly what he will say in a moment), but that empirically they do not do so. How can they? One does not clamor to embrace what one finds foolish. What they find foolish, in the context of chapters 1–2, is the message of Christ crucified, "the foolishness of what was preached to save those who believe" (1:21). These wonderful, life-transforming, redeeming things from the Spirit of God are dismissed as folly, for they are predicated on a crucified Messiah who does not easily fit into the triumphalistic biases of autonomous human beings. This is nothing other than the conclusion of 1:18–25 and of 2:10b–13.

Second, Paul insists that human beings "*cannot* understand them, because they are spiritually discerned" (2:14, emphasis added). This is the complementary truth to verse 12. There we were told that the Spirit was given to us (i.e., to believers) so "that we may understand what God has freely given us". Here Paul rules out the possibility that anyone could possibly understand this without the Spirit's aid. The focus is on our utter inability.

I remember giving a copy of John Stott's *Basic Christianity* to a bright graduate student at Cambridge University about twenty years ago. Some months later I followed up on her to find out what she had made of the book. She said she had read it right through and had been so suspicious that she had actually looked up many of the references in the Bible to make sure that the author wasn't trying to slip something past her. She had come to a conclusion: this Christianity business was OK for good people, but it wasn't for her.

Isn't that astonishing? How could an intelligent graduate student so completely miss what Stott was talking about? Somehow none of it had come together for her. The things of God remained foolishness to her, because they are spiritually discerned.

Often, of course, God uses varied and long-term means to bring about understanding. I and others talked with her at length about the gospel, and eventually she became a Christian. But I have talked with many who have not become Christians. What is the distinguishing factor between those with whom I have talked who have become believers, like this young woman, and those with whom I have talked who remain unbelievers? The ultimate distinction is in the gift of the Spirit. Various Christian workers may do their bit, but, to use the analogy that Paul himself deploys in the next chapter, a Paul may sow the seed and an Apollos may water it, but only God can make the plant grow and bring forth fruit (3:7).

What we must constantly remember is that this human inability to understand spiritual things is a *culpable* inability. It is not that God makes us constitutionally unable to understand him, and then toys with us for his own amusement. Rather, he has made us for himself, but we have run from him. The heart of our lostness is our profound self-focus. We do not *want* to know him, if knowing him is on his terms. We are happy to have a god we can more or less manipulate; we do not want a god to whom we admit that we are rebels in heart and mind, that we do not deserve his favor, and that our only hope is in his pardoning and transforming grace. We certainly cannot fathom a powerful Creator who takes the place of an odious criminal in order to save us from the judgment we deserve.

Or, more precisely, we cannot fathom such things unless we have the Spirit of God. That is what it means, in this context, to be a "spiritual man" (v. 15). The spiritual person is simply the person with the Spirit of God. The Spirit opens up entire vistas of understanding that would otherwise remain opaque to us. "The spiritual man [i.e., the person with the Spirit] makes judgments about all things, but he himself is not subject to any man's judgment" (2:15).

Unfortunately, this verse has been ripped out of its context to justify the most appalling arrogance. Some people think of them-

selves as especially spiritual and discerning Christians and judge
that this verse authorizes them, the elite of the elect, to make
well-nigh infallible judgments across a broad range of matters.
Moreover, they insist, they are so spiritual that others do not have
the right to judge them. After all, does not the apostle say that the
"spiritual man" is "not subject to any man's judgment"?

   This simply will not do. In the context, the "spiritual man" is
the person with the Holy Spirit, over against "the man without
the Spirit." The "spiritual man," in short, is the Christian, not a
member of an elite coterie of Christians. When Paul says that
"the spiritual man makes judgments about all things," in this
context he cannot possibly take "all things" absolutely—as if the
spiritual person, the Christian, is particularly equipped to judge
the scientific evidence for a particular quark or wonderfully
suited to assess the latest cortisone technique for relieving bursi-
tis. The categories of the context must prevail. "As someone has
said, 'The profane person cannot understand holiness; but the
holy person can well understand the depths of evil.' Those whose
lives are invaded by the Spirit of God can discern all things,
including those without the Spirit; but the inverse is not possible."[5] In short, when Paul says, "The spiritual man makes judgments about *all things*, but he himself is not subject to any man's
judgment" (2:15, emphasis added), "all things" covers the range
of moral and spiritual experience from the rawest paganism to
what it means to be a Christian. The Christian has lived in both
worlds and can speak of both from experience, from observation,
and from a genuine grasp of the Word of God. But the person
without the Spirit cannot properly assess what goes on in the
spiritual realm—any more than a person who is color-blind is
qualified to make nice distinctions in the dramatic hues of a sun-
set or a rainbow, any more than a person born deaf is qualified
to comment on the harmony of Beethoven's Fifth or on the voice
and technique of Pavarotti.

   It is important to think through the implications of this verse.
Christians in contemporary Western society are constantly being
told that they are ignorant, narrow, and incapable of understanding the real world. Paul says the opposite: Christians are as capa-

5. Gordon D. Fee, *The First Epistle to the Corinthians* (Grand Rapids: Eerdmans,
1987), 118.

ble as other sinners of understanding the complex and interwoven nature of sin, of grasping the ways in which "wannabe" autonomous human beings reason, and of explaining what the world looks like to modern pagans in our post-modern world. But because they have received the Spirit of God, they are also capable of saying something wise and true about the way the world appears to God. They can talk about the beauty of holiness, about God's plan of redemption and reconciliation, about the judgment to come and the nature of our desperate plight. In sum, they can talk about Christ crucified. They can talk passionately, committedly, out of the cleansing experience of being forgiven on the ground of another's death, which was offered up in love for a rebel. They can explain how great a difference that makes as they think of the future and plan their priorities. They can explore together (even if they do not always agree) what a truly Christian society would look like. And, empowered by the Spirit, they can in some measure show by their lives what such a society looks like, as redeemed men and women "are being built together to become a dwelling in which God lives by his Spirit" (Eph. 2:22). And all this makes them much more comprehensive in outlook than their pagan peers. The really narrow perspective is maintained by the sinner who has never tasted grace, by the fallen human being who has never enjoyed transforming insight, afforded by the Holy Spirit, into God's wise purposes.

From this perspective, it is idiotic—that is not too strong a word—to extol the world's perspective and secretly lust after its limited vision. That is what the Corinthians were apparently doing; that is what we are in danger of doing every time we adopt our world's shibboleths, dote on its heroes, admire its transient stars, seek its admiration, and play to its applause.

Paul brings his argument to a close with a biblical quotation drawn from Isaiah 40:13: "For who has known the mind[6] of the Lord that he may instruct him?" (1 Cor. 2:16). In Paul's context, the quotation cuts two ways. On the one hand, it is an important reminder that no one can successfully probe the depths of God's thoughts, let alone match wits with God. In our finiteness and

---

6. Although the Septuagint, the Greek Old Testament, here speaks to the mind of the Lord, this is its rendering of the Hebrew "the spirit of the Lord"—in a usage rather similar to that in 1 Corinthians 2:11.

fallenness, we will not by ourselves know the mind of the Lord. We will judge his wisdom folly; we will not assign the crucified Messiah his proper place. Unless the Spirit enlightens us, God's thoughts will remain deeply alien to us.

But on the other hand, Paul says, "we have the mind of Christ" (2:16b). This is another way of saying that we have received the Spirit of God (vv. 11–12) and have therefore understood something of God's wisdom, the wisdom of the cross. That sets us apart from the world. And therefore implicitly the world will not understand *us* either. So Paul is using this quotation from Isaiah 40 to support his claim in the preceding verse: "The spiritual man . . . is not subject to any man's judgment." He does not mean that Christians have nothing to learn from non-Christians, or that Christians are always above correction and rebuke (even from those who are not believers). He means, rather, that the mind of Christ is alien to the unbeliever, and insofar as we have the mind of Christ we will be alien to the unbeliever as well.

This passage reminds us of Jesus' words:

> If the world hates you, keep in mind that it hated me first. If you belonged to the world, it would love you as its own. As it is, you do not belong to the world, but I have chosen you out of the world. That is why the world hates you. Remember the words I spoke to you: "No servant is greater than his master." If they persecuted me, they will persecute you also. If they obeyed my teaching, they will obey yours also. They will treat you this way because of my name, for they do not know the One who sent me. [John 15:18–21]

In short, the gulf between the spiritual person and the person without the Spirit is immense; the chasm between "the world" and the people of God is unbridgeable, apart from the Spirit of God. It is therefore unbearably tragic when Christians begin to covet the plaudits of this world gone astray.

> Do not love the world or anything in the world. If anyone loves the world, the love of the Father is not in him. For everything in the world—the cravings of sinful man, the lust of his eyes and the boasting of what he has and does—comes not from the Father but from the world. The world and its desires pass away, but the man who does the will of God lives forever. [1 John 2:15–17]

Concluding Reflections

There are several important practical lessons that the church must learn from this passage. Two of them are particularly important for the contemporary Western church.

What it means to be "spiritual" is profoundly tied to the cross, and to nothing else. More precisely, to be spiritual, in this passage, is to enjoy the gift of the Holy Spirit—and this means understanding and appropriating the message of the cross, "God's secret wisdom." For Paul, being spiritual does not lead to one-upmanship, to inner circles of specially endowed saints, to spiritual elitism. In this passage there is only one fundamental division in the human race. On the one side are those without the Spirit, who are in consequence culpably ignorant of the message of the crucified Messiah; on the other side are those with the Spirit, who in consequence grasp the message of the cross.

This is not to deny that there may be gradations of maturity among the spiritual. In fact, Paul will introduce something along this line in the next chapter. But those who are more mature in the Christian way cannot claim to be "more spiritual," in the sense that they belong to a separate category of believers. They do not have the right to claim special insight beyond the grasp of ordinary Christians. The spiritual person is simply a believer, one who has closed with the message of the cross. Indeed, those who are most mature are most grateful for the cross and keep coming back to it as the measure of God's love for them and the supreme standard of personal self-denial.

Consistency demands that such a person reject the wisdom of the world and embrace "God's secret wisdom" without reservation. Where "wisdom," as in these chapters, is conceived to be a public philosophy of life and not simply healthy endowments of common sense or the like, there are only two alternatives: ultimately wisdom is from the world and is opposed by God, or it is God-given and tied to the cross. There is no middle ground. Those who try to create some middle ground by imitating the Corinthians—who confessed the Jesus of the cross but whose hearts were constantly drawn to one or another of the public philosophies and values of the day—will gain nothing but the rebuke of Scripture.

This lesson is especially important when so many Christians today identify themselves with some "single issue" (a concept drawn from politics) other than the cross, other than the gospel. It is not that they deny the gospel. If pressed, they will emphatically endorse it. But their point of self-identification, the focus of their minds and hearts, what occupies their interest and energy, is something else: a style of worship, the abortion issue, home schooling, the gift of prophecy, pop sociology, a certain brand of counseling, or whatever. Of course, all of these issues have their own importance. Doubtless we need some Christians working on them full time. But even those who are so engaged must do so as an extension of the gospel, as an extension of the message of the cross. They must take special pains to avoid giving any impression that being really spiritual or really insightful or really wise turns on an appropriate response to their issue.

I have heard a Mennonite leader assess his own movement in this way. One generation of Mennonites cherished the gospel and believed that the entailment of the gospel lay in certain social and political commitments. The next generation assumed the gospel and emphasized the social and political commitments. The present generation identifies itself with the social and political commitments, while the gospel is variously confessed or disowned; it no longer lies at the heart of the belief system of some who call themselves Mennonites.

Whether or not this is a fair reading of the Mennonites, it is certainly a salutary warning for evangelicals at large. We are already at the stage where many evangelical leaders simply assume the message of the cross, but no longer lay much emphasis on it. Their focus is elsewhere. And a few, it seems to me, are in danger of distancing themselves from major components of the message of the cross, while still operating within the context of evangelicalism. It is at least possible that we are the generation of believers who will destroy much of historic Christianity from within—not, in the first instance, by rancid unbelief, but by raising relatively peripheral questions to the place where, functionally, they displace what is central. And what shall the end of this drift be?

We must come back to the cross, and to God's plan of redemption that centers on the cross, and make that the point of our self-identification. We must consciously resist all blandishments from movements and philosophies and value systems that tolerate the cross, or even nominally promote it, but in reality displace it. We must recognize that what it means to be wise, what it means to be spiritual, is to embrace, by the help of God's Spirit, the message of the crucified Messiah.

Still, we must insist, no less strongly than Paul, that this insight into the message of the cross cannot be gained apart from the work of the Spirit. How shall we respond, then, to those who say this sounds too much like an esoteric approach to knowledge—one that can safely put aside disciplined exegesis, the words and contexts of biblical books, the hard work of study and thought, and exchange it all for some subjective claim to being led by the Spirit? Should we safeguard ourselves from this charge by siding with those who say that the Spirit does not enable us to understand the text, but simply to apply it to ourselves?

This extreme response is no less problematic than the subjectivism it seeks to avoid. Against the evil of some vague, mystical approach to biblical exegesis it restricts the role of the Spirit to mere application—though, on the face of it, 1 Corinthians 2:14 demands something stronger than that.

It will help us to think clearly about this issue if we recognize that 1 Corinthians 2 is not concerned with the mechanics of how people understand their Bibles generally, or with the quality of a particular scholar's exegesis of some specific Hebrew text. In any case, it is apparent to anyone who has read widely in the field that frequently a self-confessed unbeliever produces excellent exegesis of one passage of the Bible or another—much better than that produced by those with less training but who by the grace of God genuinely possess his Spirit. But Paul is not addressing general questions of epistemology. He is not even addressing how one comes to a knowledge of what some specific passage of Scripture really means. His focus is the fundamental message of the crucified Messiah. And this, he insists, is fundamentally incomprehensible to the mind without the Spirit.

But (someone might say) surely there are some people who can articulate the message of the cross but who don't believe it. In that sense, they do understand it; they simply do not believe it.

All they need to do is apply it to themselves. So in that case, isn't the Spirit's role reduced to mere application after all?

This, I suspect, erects a false dichotomy between understanding and application. Paul is not saying that no one among the Jews and the Gentiles of his own day understood the cross at any level. Some of them, including Paul (Saul) himself before his conversion, doubtless knew enough of what Christians believed about the cross that they could summarize it accurately. In that sense they "understood" the message of the cross. But does anyone truly understand the message of the cross apart from brokenness, contrition, repentance, and faith? To repeat rather mechanically the nature of the transaction that Christians think took place at Golgotha is one thing; to look at God and his holiness, and people and their sin, *from the perspective of the cross*, is life-changing. What Paul says, then, is that our self-centeredness, our sin, is so deep that we cannot truly see the cross for what it is, apart from the work of the Spirit. What the Spirit accomplishes in us is more than mere application of truth already grasped. Paul's point is that truly grasping the truth of the cross and being transformed cannot be separated—and both are utterly dependent on the work of the Spirit.

We see the point clearly when we ask why some today who can, formally speaking, articulate the message of the cross, do not themselves become Christians. It is, finally, because they do not think the message is true. And why not? Well, it may be because they think the message a bit barbaric. Or they may find it hard to believe that Jesus rose from the dead. Or they may construct a brand of "Christianity" full of altruism and gentleness but conclude that what the New Testament says about the crucified Messiah is an optional extra, a non essential component of "Christianity." *But in each case they can take this step only if they have bought into some philosophical or theological grid that entitles them to "filter out" the centrality of the message of the cross.* In other words, consciously or unconsciously they have bought into one of the "wisdoms" of this world and have therefore not grasped the message of the cross at all. At the deepest level, they have not really understood it. The reason for this failure does not lie in the realm of ostensibly neutral epistemology. It lies, rather, in our deep waywardness, our culpable self-interest, our alienation from God, our corresponding refusal to recognize just how lost we are. To overcome such lostness, we need the power of the Spirit of God. That is why, when it comes to grasping the message of Christ crucified, it is never a matter of "neutral" weighing of evidences.

Truly to grasp that the eternal God, our Maker and Judge, has out of inexpressible grace sent his Son to die the odious death of an abominated criminal in order that we might be forgiven and reconciled to him; that this wise plan was effected by sinful leaders who thought they were controlling events and who were operating out of selfish expediency, while in fact God was bringing about his own good, redemptive purposes; that our only hope of life in the presence of this holy and loving God lies in casting ourselves without reserve on his mercy, receiving in faith the gift of forgiveness purchased at inestimable cost—none of this is possible apart from the work of the Spirit.

And Christians say, with increasing awe and gratitude, "God has revealed it to us by his Spirit" (1 Cor. 2:10a).

Questions for Review and Reflection

1. How is this passage sometimes abused by people who take it to justify their own spiritual authority? How would you respond to such people?
2. Who are the "mature" in this chapter? Who are the "spiritual"?
3. Why does Paul here call the gospel "God's secret wisdom"? What does he mean?
4. Why must we have the Spirit of God if we are to understand the gospel?
5. Why does Paul think of Christians as broader and more knowledgeable than unbelievers? What difference should this make to your outlook on life?

3

The Cross
and Factionalism
1 Corinthians 3

¹Brothers, I could not address you as spiritual but as worldly—mere infants in Christ. ²I gave you milk, not solid food, for you were not yet ready for it. Indeed, you are still not ready. ³You are still worldly. For since there is jealousy and quarreling among you, are you not worldly? Are you not acting like mere men? ⁴For when one says, "I follow Paul," and another, "I follow Apollos," are you not mere men?

⁵What, after all, is Apollos? And what is Paul? Only servants, through whom you came to believe— as the Lord has assigned to each his task. ⁶I planted the seed, Apollos watered it, but God made it grow. ⁷So neither he who plants nor he who waters is anything, but only God, who makes things grow. ⁸The man who plants and the man who waters have one purpose, and each will be rewarded according to his own labor. ⁹For we are God's fellow workers; you are God's field, God's building.

¹⁰By the grace God has given me, I laid a foundation as an expert builder, and someone else is build-

ing on it. But each one should be careful how he builds. [11]For no one can lay any foundation other than the one already laid, which is Jesus Christ. [12]If any man builds on this foundation using gold, silver, costly stones, wood, hay or straw, [13]his work will be shown for what it is, because the Day will bring it to light. It will be revealed with fire, and the fire will test the quality of each man's work. [14]If what he has built survives, he will receive his reward. [15]If it is burned up, he will suffer loss; he himself will be saved, but only as one escaping through the flames.

[16]Don't you know that you yourselves are God's temple and that God's Spirit lives in you? [17]If anyone destroys God's temple, God will destroy him; for God's temple is sacred, and you are that temple.

[18]Do not deceive yourselves. If any one of you thinks he is wise by the standards of this age, he should become a "fool" so that he may become wise. [19]For the wisdom of this world is foolishness in God's sight. As it is written: "He catches the wise in their craftiness"; [20]and again, "The Lord knows that the thoughts of the wise are futile." [21]So then, no more boasting about men! All things are yours, [22]whether Paul or Apollos or Cephas or the world or life or death or the present or the future—all are yours, [23]and you are of Christ, and Christ is of God.

Few passages of the New Testament have been abused by preachers and writers more than this one.

First, large branches of Christendom have appealed to this chapter to support a doctrine of purgatory. Unlike hell, the experience of purgatory is said to be temporary. Believers with unconfessed sin go there to suffer for awhile until God judges that they are ready for heaven. Such a person will be saved, "but only as one escaping through the flames" (1 Cor. 3:15). This is the only passage in the New Testament that has even a remote chance of supporting a doctrine of purgatory, so what we understand it to mean is clearly important. Generally speaking, those who adhere to a doctrine of purgatory rest much of the weight of their argument not on the Old or New Testaments, but on apocryphal books and church tradition.

Second (and more commonly in evangelicalism, especially American evangelicalism), some appeal to this passage for a threefold division of the human race. At one end is the "natural man" (KJV), the person without the Spirit (2:14), the unregenerate. At the other end is the "spiritual man" (2:15), the Christian who is walking with the Lord in joyful obedience and fruitfulness. In between is the "carnal" man (KJV; "worldly" in the NIV, 3:1–4), the person who is a Christian and who is assured of heaven, but who is living a life indistinguishable from the world. Such a person, we are told, "will be saved, but only as one escaping through the flames." Whatever work he or she has done "is burned up"; such people "suffer loss" (3:15).

At a superficial level, this interpretation sounds plausible enough, until one observes (as we shall) that verse 15, which talks about suffering loss and escaping through the flames, does not apply such language to the "worldly" person or the "carnal" Christian at all. Certainly there is such a thing as a carnal or worldly Christian, but the "carnal Christian" theory has in recent years taken on some fairly weird extremes that bear little relation to what this chapter actually says. When we remember that this is the only place where the New Testament uses this language, we are forced to recognize that it is important to get the interpretation of the passage right.

Two preliminary observations will start us off on the right course.

1. This chapter, 1 Corinthians 3, is part of one sustained argument that runs from 1:10 to 4:21. Primarily, Paul addresses the deep divisiveness, the wretched factionalism, that plagues the church at Corinth. Certain people from Chloe's household have informed him how some in the church say, "I follow Paul," or "I follow Apollos"—or someone else. That theme is still tripping along in this chapter (see vv. 5–6, 21–23) and continues on into chapter 4 (see 4:6). That the problem of factionalism was deeply rooted in the Corinthian church is probably supported by the fact that Paul felt the need to enlarge upon the nature and centrality of love (1 Cor. 13) as the Christian way, the "most excellent way" (1 Cor. 12:31). So however we interpret 1 Corinthians 3, it must fit into the developing argument the apostle advances from 1:10 to 4:21.

2. Although Paul directly addresses the bitter factionalism of the Corinthian believers in these chapters, he does so in part by tackling two deeper problems that lie behind the factionalism and undergird it. The first is the Corinthians' implicit misunderstanding of the gospel, and in particular of the centrality of the cross. Pragmatically, their love of pomp, prestige, rhetoric, social approval, publicly lauded "wisdom"—in short, their raw triumphalism—demonstrated that they had not reflected very deeply on the entailments of the gospel of the crucified Messiah. That is why Paul spends so much time on these points in the first two chapters of his epistle. But the second implicit misunderstanding displayed by these squabbling Corinthians concerned the nature of Christian leadership. As long as some Christians are saying, "I am of Paul [or Apollos, or Cephas, or Wesley, or Calvin]," making some Christian leader the prime point of their identification, they do not truly grasp the nature of Christian leadership. Clearing up these misapprehensions is what largely occupies the apostle in 1 Corinthians 3–4.

Paul hammers home three points in the first of these two chapters.

Factionalists Display Marks of Wretched, Unacceptable, Spiritual Immaturity (3:1–4)

Although Paul is about to berate the Corinthians in a devastating manner, not for a moment does he think that they are not Christians at all. After all, they have the Spirit of God, the mind of Christ, as he has just finished explaining in chapter 2. For Paul, that is the touchstone: "if anyone does not have the Spirit of Christ, he does not belong to Christ" (Rom. 8:9). At heart, therefore, they really have grasped the message of Christ crucified, even if they have not brought their lives into conformity with this message. Moreover, Paul wants the Corinthian believers to recognize that this is how he thinks of them. That is why he now addresses them as "brothers" (3:1).

But although he does not tell his readers that they do not have the Spirit, what he does say is shocking: "Brothers, I could not address you as *spiritual* [i.e., as those with the Spirit]" (3:1, emphasis added). Instead, Paul had to address them "as worldly."

The Greek word behind "worldly" is *sarkinos*, literally "fleshly." (The word Paul regularly uses for "flesh" is *sarx*.) The Latin equivalent of "fleshly," rendered into English, is "carnal," the word used in the King James Version. And that is how we have come to speak of the "carnal Christian." There is no doubt there is such a thing. But what is a "carnal Christian," a "worldly Christian"? It will help us to see what Paul means if we take four steps.

First, in modern English the expression *carnal Christian* is potentially misleading. The word carnal has come to be associated with sexual sin (there is no doubt what "carnal desire" means today)—and at this juncture Paul is certainly not accusing the Corinthians of lust or of sexual misconduct. That is probably why the translators of the New International Version chose *worldly* to render *sarkinos*: it suggests a broader failure than the merely sexual.

Second, the word *sarkinos* itself simply means something like "made of flesh"—that is, merely human. The same word is found in 2 Corinthians 3:3, where Paul tells us that under the new covenant the letter of Christ is written "not on tablets of stone but on tablets of *human* hearts" (emphasis added)—literally, "hearts *of flesh*." Certainly in this latter passage there is no necessary overtone of evil. So what Paul is saying in 1 Corinthians 3:1, therefore, is that he discovered he could not address the Corinthians "as spiritual" (that is, as people with the Spirit) but would have to speak with them as "fleshly" (that is, as people without the Spirit).

So although on the one hand Paul believes his readers possess the Spirit, and therefore he calls them "brothers," on the other hand he feels he cannot address them as people with the Spirit. That is why he has had to rearticulate the elementary gospel to them again in the first two chapters of this epistle. So what are they? Are they people with the Spirit, or not? Are they Christians, or not? Paul explains his paradoxical use of language: they are "mere infants in Christ" (3:1). Yes, they are Christians; yes, they do have the Spirit. But in certain particulars, still to be laid out, they simply do not act like it. Paul judges them to be spiritually immature—wretchedly, unacceptably, spiritually immature. "I gave you milk, not solid food," he adds, "for you were not yet ready for it. Indeed, you are still not ready" (3:2).

When my daughter was born, my wife found herself unable to nurse our infant. That gave me the privilege of sharing the midnight feedings. Tiffany was a dream: I could zap the formula in the microwave, change her, feed her the whole eight ounces, and tuck her back into her crib—all in under twenty minutes. Then our son came along. Midnight feedings with him were horrendous. Although he had an enormous appetite, he sucked and drank with only three speeds: slow, dead-slow, and stop. Worse, he had to be burped every ounce or so—a painfully slow process—or he would display his remarkable gift for projectile vomiting. Without any warning, he could upchuck what he had taken in and send it fifteen feet across the room. If there were an Olympic event in projectile vomiting, he would have taken one of the medals. I never got him back into his crib in under an hour; an hour and a half was more common.

At least he had an excuse. He was young, and his digestive system was obviously not as well-developed as his sister's at the same age. Best of all, he quickly outgrew this stage. But there are Christians who are international-class projectile vomiters, spiritually speaking, after years and years of life. They simply cannot digest what Paul calls "solid food." You must give them milk, for they are not ready for anything more. And if you try to give them anything other than milk, they upchuck and make a mess of everyone and everything around them. At some point the number of years they have been Christians leads you to expect something like mature behavior from them, but they prove disappointing. They are infants still and display their wretched immaturity even in the way that they complain if you give them more than milk. Not for them solid knowledge of Scripture; not for them mature theological reflection; not for them growing and perceptive Christian thought. They want nothing more than another round of choruses and a "simple message"—something that won't challenge them to think, to examine their lives, to make choices, and to grow in their knowledge and adoration of the living God.

So the Corinthians, then, are wretchedly immature believers.

Third, this immaturity is something for which they will be held accountable. Unlike my son, who could not help his condition, these people Paul holds responsible for their "worldliness." This Paul makes clear even by a small change in vocabulary from verse 1 to verse 3. The word behind "worldly" in verse 1, as we have seen, is *sarkinos*. In the two occurrences of "worldly" in verse 3, the word is *sarkikos*. If there is a difference in meaning between the two words, it is this: while *sarkinos* means "made of flesh" or "composed of flesh" (and thus refers to those who are acting as if they did not have the Spirit, but are merely human, "fleshly"), *sarkikos* means something like "characteristic of human flesh." In other words, this word immediately takes on moral overtones. Human life apart from the Spirit of God is not neutral; it has certain characteristics that are entirely reprehensible. This meaning of *sarkikos* is made clear from its use in 2 Corinthians 1:12, where Paul testifies, "we have conducted ourselves . . . not according to *worldly* wisdom but according to God's grace" (emphasis added). In other words, Paul has behaved not in line with the "wisdom" that reflects the point of view of sinful human nature, but in line with God's grace. Similarly, in 1 Corinthians 3:3 Paul tells the Corinthians that they are acting in ways that are characteristic of people without the Spirit—of people who, precisely because they do not have the Spirit, have nothing to fall back on but their own sinful human nature, their "fleshly" nature. They are acting like pagans.

Fourth, Paul gives some content to his charge. It is very important to grasp what evidence Paul adduces to support his conclusion that the Corinthian believers are worldly. One bit of evidence we have already looked at: Paul finds the Corinthians stuck at the "milk" stage. They are not growing in their understanding and application of the Word of God generally, and of the gospel in particular. But now he adds two more pieces of evidence, and they are related to each other. (1) The Corinthian believers display "jealousy and quarreling" (3:3). As long as they manifest such sins, they are worldly (*sarkikos*), exhibiting what is characteristic of fallen human nature. They are "acting like mere men" (3:3), that is, as if they did not have the Spirit. (2) The Corinthian believers have succumbed to factionalism, one group claiming to follow Paul, another group associating itself with the name of Apollos, another with Peter, and so forth (1:11–12; 3:4). This factionalism and all the petty animosities it engenders are characteristic of "mere men"—not of men and women who possess the Spirit of the living God.

So this is what Paul means by a "worldly" Christian, by a "carnal" Christian (if we adopt older English). Paul does not have in mind someone who has made a profession of faith, carried on in the Christian way for a short while, and then reverted to a lifestyle indistinguishable in every respect from that of the world. After all, these Corinthian believers are meeting together for worship (1 Cor. 14), they call on the name of the Lord Jesus Christ (1:2), they are extraordinarily endowed with spiritual gifts (1:5, 7; 12–14), they are wrestling with theological and ethical issues (1 Cor. 8–10), and they are in contact with the apostle whose ministry brought them to the Lord. Far from being sold out to the world, the flesh, and the devil, they pursue spiritual experience, if sometimes unwisely.

Of course, if professing Christians slip far enough, some further category has to be found for them. Paul has one. In 2 Corinthians, after he has discovered that the Corinthian church, despite temporary restoration, has succumbed yet again to false apostles (2 Cor. 11:13) and to a lifestyle that does not glory in the cross (2 Cor. 10-13), Paul finally feels forced to this extreme injunction: "Examine yourselves to see whether you are in the faith; test yourselves. Do you not realize that Christ Jesus is in you—unless, of course, you fail the test?" (2 Cor. 13:5). In other words, if their drift away from the gospel becomes serious enough, Paul questions whether they are Christians at all. And this takes place at a point when the Corinthian congregation is still holding together as professing Christians.

What this means is that it will not do to apply "carnal Christian" or "worldly Christian" to every person who has made a profession of faith, perhaps years ago, but who for umpteen years has lived without any evidence of Christian faith, life, repentance, values, or interest. In such instances it is far more likely than not that we are dealing with spurious conversions.

Once this is clear, Paul's point becomes potent. Those who have the Spirit, and who therefore come to grips with the message of the cross (1 Cor. 2), are expected to mature rapidly. Such maturation will disclose itself in a growing ability to take in more and more Christian truth (3:2). It will also show itself in a large-hearted attitude that avoids quarreling and jealousy, and refuses to sink into narrow factionalism. If some who have the Spirit are slow to display this rising maturity, the kindest interpretation is that they are "worldly." In these matters they are acting like "mere men" instead of like Christian men and women, men and women empowered by the Spirit of God. They are wretchedly, unacceptably, spiritually immature.

Factionalists Ignore Two Important Truths about Christian Leaders (3:5–17)

The two truths can be simply set out:

1. Christian leaders are only servants of Christ and are not to be accorded allegiance reserved for God alone.

2. God cares about his church, and he holds its leaders accountable for how they build it.

No less interesting than these two truths is the way Paul establishes them. He makes his points by painting two analogies, an agricultural one (3:5–9a) and an architectural one (3:9b–15), following them up with a powerful rhetorical question and an alarming conclusion (3:16–17).

The Agricultural Analogy (3:5–9a)

Having berated the Corinthian Christians for their spiritual immaturity, attested by their squabbling and fractious attachment to particular human leaders, Paul judges it necessary to say something about how such leaders should be viewed. "What, after all, is Apollos? And what is Paul?" (3:5). The answer is devastatingly simple: "Only servants, through whom you came to believe—as the Lord has assigned to each his task" (3:5). Christian leaders are, in the first place, "only servants." In this context, Paul does not mean "servants of the church," but "servants of Jesus Christ," for here it is the Lord who "has assigned to each his task." Moreover, they are specifically called "servants of Christ" in 1 Corinthians 4:1. If the Lord Jesus himself "has assigned to each his task," it is idiotic to rank them according to their jobs. These servants have not gained their status by ambition and "natural gift" (as if in God's world there can be any gift that he himself has not given!), but by the specific assignment of the Lord. Discharging the responsibilities assigned them, they have become the agents who brought the Corinthians to faith—"servants [of Christ], through whom you came to believe" (3:5).

Now the agricultural analogy is laid out. In a large farm, one person may sow the seed and another may water it, but only God can make it grow. To heap unqualified and exclusive praise on the sower is to focus too narrowly; to praise those who handle the irrigation and forget those who sow the seed is to be myopic. In any case it is God alone who makes things grow. Should not he be praised?

Even though the workers are assigned different tasks, they "have one purpose" (3:8). No one worker's task has any independent importance. It is in the bringing together of the tasks, crowned by God himself who makes things grow, that the harvest is finally brought in. Doubtless each worker "will be rewarded according to his own labor." Paul does not want to deny the importance of individual faithfulness and industry. But in terms of the great task at hand—making things grow and bringing them to harvest—it is important to get the big picture straight. "We are God's fellow workers" (3:9), Paul writes. He does not mean that he and Apollos and others are co-workers with God, as if he, Apollos, other workers, and God are all on the same level. Rather, he means that he and Apollos and any other workers are simply fellow workers, co-workers, owned by God, used by God. The word *God's* is here possessive. We are fellow workers, Paul says, and we are God's. Clearly, as far as Paul is concerned, to be a servant of Jesus Christ and to be one of God's workers amounts to the same thing.

The entire sweep of the analogy now becomes clear. The field represents the Corinthians, and it belongs to God ("you are God's field," 3:9); the workers in the field are people like Paul and Apollos, and they belong to God ("we are God's fellow workers," 3:9). God owns the field and the workers; he assigns the workers their task, and he alone makes the seed grow.

Before we press on to the next analogy, we must make sure that two points of the agricultural analogy are clear. The first is that the analogy as a whole strongly sets out one of the two truths that the Corinthians are ignoring: Christian leaders are only servants of Christ and are not to be accorded allegiance that is reserved for God alone. It is not that gratitude to Paul or Apollos or some other worker is inappropriate. Rather, what Paul finds inexcusable is the kind of fawning and defensive attachment to one particular leader that results in one-upmanship, quarreling, and jealousy. Implicitly, such allegiance is making too much of one person. It verges on assigning that person godlike status. In fact, a little sober reflection reminds us that many Christian leaders properly contribute to our spiritual growth and fruitfulness, but in any case it is God alone who gives life and fruitfulness, however much he uses means. No Christian leader is to be venerated or listened to or adulated with the kind of allegiance and devotion properly reserved for God alone. That is folly; it betrays a deep ignorance of the nature of true Christian leadership and of the corporate and mutually supportive ways in which Christian leaders complement one another's work under God. Implicitly, of course (though Paul has not yet made the point), this also means that Christian leaders should refrain from presenting themselves as if they had the corner on the truth, or all the gifts, or exclusive authority or insight. We are all "only servants." We are "fellow workers," and we are God's.

The second detail we must observe from this analogy is that the entire thrust of the argument depends on a distinction between the Corinthian believers and Christian workers such as Paul and Apollos. That is made clear not only from the context, in which groups of Corinthian believers are trying to align themselves with specific leaders, but from the structure of the analogy: "*we* [that is, Paul, Apollos, and, in principle, other workers] are God's fellow workers; *you* are God's field" (3:9, emphasis added). In other contexts, of course, Paul can talk of all Christians as serving the Lord, as being his servants. But in this context, it is essential to Paul's argument to maintain the distinction. That distinction, we shall see, carries over to the next analogy—and this is a crucial factor in the proper interpretation of the passage.

The Architectural Analogy (3:9b–15)

The end of verse 9 is transitional. "You are God's field," Paul writes, bringing the agricultural analogy to a close. And then he adds, "[you are] God's building." So we move from the farm to the construction site. Once again a distinction is maintained between the "ordinary" believers and the leaders. Here the believers are "God's building"; the leaders are the builders.

The general point of this analogy, especially the first part of it, is exactly the same as that of the agricultural analogy. We will understand it better if we remember what a slow process building a great edifice was before the days of power equipment. Cathedrals in Europe often took four or five centuries to complete, sometimes longer. In Paul's day, a temple, a much more modest edifice than a medieval cathedral, sometimes took decades. So one builder might lay the foundation; others would complete various phases of the building project and then would move on, retire, or die, while still others would take their places. The lesson is clear: Paul laid the foundation, and others have built on his work. It is the project as a whole that is important, and, implicitly, it is foolish to focus all praise on just one of the builders who has contributed to the project. The builders themselves, after all, have shared a common vision, a common purpose.

But there are two elements to this analogy that differentiate it from the previous one, and these are related. The first is that God plays a rather different role in the two "parables." In the agricultural analogy, God is represented by the owner of the field who also employs the workers; moreover, God is praised as the One who alone gives life: he makes the crops grow. Here, however, in the analogy drawn from the building industry, there is nothing organic, there is nothing growing, and so God necessarily plays a somewhat different role. Jesus Christ himself becomes the foundation that Paul laid (3:11). God is not specifically mentioned in verses 11 through 15, but he stands behind the judgment implicit in "the Day" and "the fire" that will reveal the quality of each builder's work. In other words, God owns the building, and he judges the quality of the work of each builder. This point becomes explicit in 3:16–17, as we shall see.

The second element that distinguishes this analogy from the previous one is the heavy emphasis placed on the accountability of the builders. Paul no sooner gets going than he warns, "But each one should be careful how he builds" (3:10b). He himself "laid a foundation as an expert builder," and "no one can lay any foundation other than the one already laid, which is Jesus Christ"

(3:10–11). If what is being built is the church of God, the only possible foundation is Jesus Christ, or, more fully, "Jesus Christ and him crucified," to use the expression of 2:2. Paul is still thinking of the exclusive power, wisdom, and authority bound up with the gospel. If anyone tries to lay down some other foundation, then it must be for some other building. It is certainly not the church that will rise on any competing foundation.

But even where the foundation is "Jesus Christ and him crucified," there is the danger of later shoddy workmanship and inferior materials. Builders may use "gold, silver, costly stones, wood, hay or straw" (3:12). Paul does not make anything of this descending scale of values. Rather, he distinguishes between only two kinds of building materials: the kind that cannot withstand the fire that "will test the quality of each man's work" on "the Day" when each builder's work "will be shown for what it is" (3:13), and the kind that survives. "The Day" is the day of the Lord, the time of final sifting; "the fire" distinguishes good and bad. As frequently in the Old Testament, fire consumes the dross and leaves the precious metal. At first glance we might think that "gold, silver, [and] costly stones" are strange building materials. Probably Paul has chosen them not only because they will pass unscathed through fire (gold, for example, may melt, but it is still gold, no more and no less), but also because gold, silver, and precious stones featured so prominently in the building of Solomon's temple. And, as Paul develops his analogy here, the building that is going up is nothing less than "God's temple" (3:16).

This fire, then, is not purgatory. Nothing is said about tormenting the builders and purging them in the flames. Rather, it is the quality of their work that is revealed by the fire. If a builder's work is burned up, "he will suffer loss; he himself will be saved, but only as one escaping through the flames" (3:15). The picture is of someone running out of a building engulfed in a great fire. That person escapes. But how much of the building on which he has been working survives the flames?

Two things must be said to clarify this picture Paul has painted and to drive his points home into our lives. First, those who "suffer loss" but who escape "through the flames" are not the "carnal" or "worldly" Christians of 3:1–4, but are Christian leaders who build the church with materials that will not withstand the final conflagration. The worldly Christians of 3:1–4 constitute all or part of the Corinthian church, and the church is represented, in the first analogy, by the field, and in the second, by the building. What we might call the "church builders," people like Paul, Apollos, and other evangelists, preachers, and teachers, are either the workers in the field or the builders of the building. It is they whose work is tested by fire.

This means that the sophisticated form of the "carnal Christian" theory, which postulates that some people make a profession of faith, shortly thereafter return to a lifestyle indistinguishable from that of any unbeliever, yet finally make it into heaven by the skin of their teeth ("as one escaping through the flames"), finds no warrant whatever in this passage. Even the "worldly" or "carnal" Christian is still identifiably a Christian, and in this passage it is the church builders who barely escape the flames, not the "ordinary" church folk themselves.

This ought to be extremely sobering to all who are engaged in vocational ministry. It is possible to "build the church" with such shoddy materials that at the last day you have nothing to show for your labor. People may come, feel "helped," join in corporate worship, serve on committees, teach Sunday school classes, bring their friends, enjoy "fellowship," raise funds, participate in counseling sessions and self-help groups, but still not really know the Lord. If the church is being built with large portions of charm, personality, easy oratory, positive thinking, managerial skills, powerful and emotional experiences, and people smarts, but without the repeated, passionate, Spirit-anointed proclamation of "Jesus Christ and him crucified," we may be winning more adherents than converts. Not for a moment am I suggesting that, say, managerial skills are unnecessary, or that basic people skills are merely optional. But the fundamental nonnegotiable, that without which the church is no longer the church, is the gospel, God's "folly," Jesus Christ and him crucified.

If we see this clearly, then many other things will fall into place. We will perceive that it is God's revelation to us of his Son that is of paramount importance. Recognizing the need for the Spirit of God to illumine the minds of men and women who otherwise will not grasp the gospel, we will emphasize prayer. We will live and serve in the light of the final judgment, for we must give an account of our ministry. It is not that we shall refuse any practical help from those who have something to say about technique or sociological profiles; rather, we will remain utterly committed to the centrality of the cross, not just at vague, theoretical levels, but in all our strategy and practical decisions. We will be fearful of adopting approaches that might empty the cross of Christ of its power (1:17), and the only approval we shall seek is his who tests the quality of each builder's work on the last day.

Second, the prospects before the builders of the church are not merely negative. There is an alternative: "If what he has built survives, he will receive his reward" (3:14, emphasis added). Some Christians are constantly afraid that any mention of rewards will jeopardize the freedom of grace. They ignore not only that Jesus promised rewards to his followers (e.g., Matt. 6:4, 6, 18), but that the passage before us prepares the ground for the notion. Already in the agricultural analogy we are told that each worker "will be rewarded according to his own labor" (3:8). In the analogy drawn from the building industry, God is the One who judges the quality of each builder's labor—and in principle that opens up the possibility not only of loss but of reward.

It is important to recognize that Paul found it necessary to combat two extremes. On the one hand, many forms of Hellenistic religion bought into an enormous dichotomy between "spirituality" and conduct. Individuals could be ever so "pious," ever so "religious," ever so "spiritual," without it making a scrap of difference to their ethics, to their daily conduct. By contrast, believers depicted in the Bible, whether under the old covenant or the new, could not allow themselves to think that way. In the Bible, spirituality and ethics go hand in hand; piety and conduct cannot be divorced. There are consequences to our beliefs and spiritual commitments, and these pertain not only to this life but also to the life to come. So Paul's emphasis on reward was an important safeguard against the sheer libertinism of much first-century Hellenistic religion.

But on the other hand, some forms of Judaism tended to tie rewards rather tightly to the quality of one's personal obedience. Sooner or later, it becomes difficult to avoid some brand of "merit theology." But for Paul, "wages" are not credited "as an obligation" (Rom. 4:4); they are the result of grace. If Paul worked hard, it was because of God's grace in his life: "But by the grace of God I am what I am, and his grace to me was not without effect. No, I worked harder than all of them—yet not I, but the grace of God that was with me" (1 Cor. 15:10). That God's grace empowers our works destroys all mechanical merit theology: so much work, so much pay. At the end of the day, we work and serve with the end in view and constantly remember that if we are fruitful it is because God's grace is at work within us. We work out our own salvation but must remember that this is God at work within us, enabling us both to will and to act according to his good purpose (Phil. 2:12–13). This stance enables Paul to avoid legalism.

By now it should be clear that this second analogy, based on the building industry, establishes not only the first important truth that the Corinthians were ignoring (Christian leaders are only servants of Christ and are not to be accorded allegiance reserved for God alone.), but also the second major truth: God cares about his church, and he holds its leaders accountable. That is a desperately important lesson. If leaders are too greatly elevated in the popular mind, they can do almost anything, and large numbers of their followers will trail along unquestioningly. We marvel how many educated Germans followed Adolf Hitler without protest; we marvel how many religious people followed Jim Jones to their death. But examples that are not so extreme may be more difficult to detect. It is possible so to lionize some Christian leader that we start making excuses for his or her serious, perhaps even catastrophic, faults. What we must remember is that the leaders are no more than servants. Meanwhile, God loves his church, and he holds accountable those who seek to build the church.

These points are powerfully brought home in the next verses.

Paul's Rhetorical Question and His Alarming Conclusion (3:16–17)

"Don't you know that you yourselves are God's temple and that God's Spirit lives in you?" (3:16), Paul asks. The building now clearly becomes "God's temple." It is crucial to understand that in this context "God's temple" does not refer to the human body, but to the church. Elsewhere, the same metaphor is used to foster sexual purity in the individual human being (1 Cor. 6:19): if "your body is a temple of the Holy Spirit," it is important to keep that temple pure. But here in 1 Corinthians 3 that is not the issue. Paul is not saying, "Look here, if God's Spirit takes up residence in the body of the individual Christian, it is important not to contaminate that body with sexual sin, indolence, bad habits," or whatever. Rather, he is saying something like this: "Haven't you grasped that the Spirit of God animates the body of Christ on earth, the church, the community of the redeemed? *That* is the 'building,' the 'temple,' on which all the builders have been working. And you must understand that God loves the church and jealously guards it as the dwelling place of his own Spirit." But there is an entailment: "If anyone destroys God's temple, God will destroy him; for God's temple is sacred, and you are that temple" (3:17).

In the light of the immediately preceding verses, this warning is surely directed, in the first place, against builders who have resorted to combustible materials (wood, hay, stubble) that cannot withstand the fire on the last day. But it is quite possible that Paul's generous language opens up the warning to apply to others than leaders alone. After all, he does not now say, "If any *builder* destroys God's temple . . ." but "If *anyone* destroys God's temple . . ." (emphasis added). By such inclusive language Paul may be considering the kind of damage being done to God's temple, the church, by the Corinthians themselves. By diverting attention away from the gospel while focusing on the plaudits and approval of the world and its "wisdom," the Corinthian believers are in danger of undermining the very message that called the church into existence.

The ways of destroying the church are many and colorful. Raw factionalism will do it. Rank heresy will do it. Taking your eyes off the cross and letting other, more peripheral matters dominate the agenda will do it—admittedly more slowly than frank heresy, but just as effectively on the long haul. Building the church with superficial "conversions" and wonderful programs that rarely bring people into a deepening knowledge of the living God will do it. Entertaining people to death but never fostering the beauty of holiness or the centrality of self-crucifying love will build an assembly of religious people, but it will destroy the church of the living God. Gossip, prayerlessness, bitterness, sustained biblical illiteracy, self-promotion, materialism—all of these things, and many more, can destroy a church. And to do so is dangerous: "If anyone destroys God's temple, God will destroy him; for God's temple is sacred, and you are that temple" (1 Cor. 3:17). It is a fearful thing to fall into the hands of the living God.

These kinds of truths the factionalists of Corinth ignored. And these truths are all too frequently ignored by their modern counterparts. This calls for thoughtful self-examination and quiet repentance.

Factionalists Ignore the Wealth of the Heritage We as Christians Properly Enjoy (3:18–23)

The first part of this paragraph in 1 Corinthians 3 (18–21a) pauses for a review. Paul returns to the contrast between the wisdom of the world and the wisdom of God, between the foolishness of the world and the foolishness of God. But although Paul is, in part, reviewing one of his central themes in these chapters, he is also leading us into fresh thought. He begins with a warning. In the light of the fact that God cares about his temple and holds to account those who destroy it, Paul sternly writes, "Do not deceive yourselves" (3:18). Do not think that you can adopt the philosophies and values of the world as if such choices do not have a profoundly detrimental impact on the church. Do not think you can get away with it. Do not kid yourself that you are with it, an avant-garde Christian, when in fact you are leaving the gospel behind and doing damage to God's church.

The path of true wisdom, as Paul has already explained in detail in the first two chapters of this epistle, is to side with God. There one discovers that the Almighty utterly reverses so many of the values cherished by the world. What the world judges wise, God dismisses as folly; what the world rejects as foolishness is nothing less than God's wisdom. The world loves power and prestige; God displays himself most tellingly on the cross, in sublime and wretched weakness—yet that "weakness" effects God's utterly breathtaking redemptive plan, and thus proves stronger than all the world's "strength." The world pants after strong leaders, but leaders in the church must first of all be servants of the Lord Christ. The world parades its heroes and gurus; Christians remember that God loves to choose the weak and the lowly and the despised—the nobodies—so that no one may boast before him. The world tries to impress with its rhetoric and sophistication, cherishing form more than content. The apostles of Jesus Christ prize truth above style and quietly refuse to endorse any form that may prove so attractive, even diversionary, that the centrality of gospel truth is jeopardized.

That is the kind of great reversal that anyone who understands the cross must come to grips with. "If any one of you thinks he is wise by the standards of this age, he should become a 'fool' so that he may become wise. For the wisdom of this world is foolishness in God's sight" (3:18b–19a). Paul has not only returned us to the themes of chapter 1, but, in the light of his intervening discussion, he has invested them with a powerful new emphasis. Don't kid yourself, Paul says; part of what it means to be a Christian is to side with God's values in this great reversal. And be assured that God knows your heart and is never deceived; still less is he outsmarted by human plots and pretensions. "As it is written: 'He catches the wise in their craftiness' [citing Job 5:13]; and again, 'The Lord knows that the thoughts of the wise are futile' [citing Ps. 94:11]" (1 Cor. 3:19b–20).

The immediate application of this exhortation is the frank prohibition of factionalism: "So then, no more boasting about men!" (3:21a). To boast about some hero or guru is wrong for two reasons. It is wrong because the focus is wrong; the concentration is on some human being and not on the Lord God. The agricultural analogy has reminded us that God alone assigns the task, and God alone gives life; therefore God alone should be praised. The analogy from the building industry reminds us that God is the Judge, and he deeply cares what kind of edifice, what kind of "temple," we are putting up. He holds the builders accountable for their work—and, in principle, he threatens to destroy *anyone* who destroys his temple. So why should we be boasting about our attachment to some particular builder? Paul has already defended the simpler, more fundamental priority: "Let him who boasts boast in the Lord" (1:31). Now the negative corollary is put forward: "So then, no more boasting about men!" (3:21a).

But the second reason why it is wrong to boast about some human leader or other is that it cuts you off from the wider heritage that is rightfully yours. You may be boasting because you think you have the best part; in fact, you are robbing yourself, because you are restricting yourself to only one part of the heritage that is yours in Christ Jesus.

That is Paul's point in the closing lines of this paragraph: "All things are yours, whether Paul or Apollos or Cephas or the world or life or death or the present or the future—all are yours, and you are of Christ, and Christ is of God" (3:21b–23). Part of the meaning of this sentence is clear enough. Paul, Apollos, Cephas (and, in principle, any other bona fide leader in the church) all contribute to the church. They belong to the church, in exactly the same way that the farm workers all belong to the field and its harvest, and the contractors and builders all belong to the building project. To focus on one part of the project as if it were everything is to cut oneself off from the project as a whole. To fasten undue and exclusive affection and loyalty on one leader is to depreciate how much there is to receive from all the others. In other words, factionalists overlook the wealth of the heritage we as Christians properly enjoy.

But Paul casts this truth in a form that goes beyond people. "All things are yours," he says. And in the list that follows, although he begins with Paul, Apollos, and Cephas, he then adds, "or the world or life or death or the present or the future—all are yours, and you are of Christ, and Christ is of God." What does he mean?

The five things that follow "Paul or Apollos or Cephas" represent the fundamental tyrannies of human life, the things that enslave us, the things that hold us in bondage. (1) The *world* squeezes us into its mold (compare Rom. 12:1–2). It demands so much of our attention and allegiance that we seldom devote thought and passion to the world to come. *This* world ties us down; it does not encourage us to soar into the unexplored dimensions of the new heaven and the new earth. (2) Similarly, this present *life* clamors to be treated as if it were worthy of ultimate respect. We cling to life as if the Bible had never told us that our lives are but vapor that quickly vanishes when the first puff of breeze passes by. We forget that Jesus told us not to fear those who can take away *this* life, but to fear him, rather, "who can destroy both soul and body in hell" (Matt. 10:28). So where is the wisdom in endlessly serving the noisy pressures of this life if we take no thought for the life to come? And at the end of this life, there is only (3) *death*, which hovers over us, the ultimate specter. Death is a tyranny that no one escapes. Its power extends far beyond the mere experience of it. Because it looms just over the horizon, it casts its long shadow backward and constrains us all our lives. Even the attempt to live our lives by suppressing the thought of death is an abysmal response that mutely attests the power of its tyranny. So also does our habit of setting "life goals," on the morbid assumption that all we have is threescore years and ten, more or less. How would our life goals change if we were planning not only for seventy years of existence here, but also for eternity? Isn't this partly what Jesus meant when he told us to lay up treasure in heaven (Matt. 6:19–21)? But we find it very hard to heed his admonition, because death tyrannizes us. (4) Thus the constant urgency of the *present* and (5) the vague promises and threats of the *future* combine to divert our attention away from the God who holds both the present and the future in his hands.

For that, surely, is Paul's point. If we truly belong to Christ, and Christ belongs to God, then we belong to God. And what a God! He is sovereign over these petty tyrannies; he has shown his great love to his people; he has paid for their redemption at the cost of the death of his dear Son. All five realities look very different if we examine them from the secure position of belonging to Jesus Christ. (1) This *world* becomes the gateway to the next. Here God has placed us, and, recognizing his sovereign sway, we delight in the good gifts he has given us here, even as we recognize that allegiance to Christ means we can no longer "belong" to the fallen order in rebellion against its Maker. No, we do not belong to it anymore; but in one important sense, this world belongs to us. Everything belongs to our heavenly Father, and we are his children; so everything belongs to us. Of course, the world is not "ours" for our ruthless and selfish exploitation. It is "ours" only in connection with our relationship to our God and Father. But that means we belong to the One who will one day create a new heaven and earth and will enable us to delight in it. We are the heirs of God; we are coheirs with Christ (Rom. 8:17). If we suffer in this world, as he did, it is a relatively trifling matter, considering that God in his grace has joined us to the "winning side." We can no longer be tyrannized by this world, for its sway is not absolute; our allegiance belongs to another, and our vision is cast beyond this world to the world to come.

Similar things can be said about the other four tyrannies. (2) This present *life* is no longer merely something to cling to. It is the sphere in which we may serve our God and Redeemer, in anticipation of the life to come. (3) *Death*, that fearsome "last enemy" (1 Cor. 15:26), cannot have the last word, for our Master has vanquished death. His resurrection presages our own. At one level death can even be embraced, for, with Paul, we recognize that to be away from the body is to be at home with the Lord (2 Cor. 5:8). We even understand what Paul meant when he said, "For to me, to live is Christ and to die is gain" (Phil. 1:21). (4) The *present* is where I live and serve God, but it cannot devour me. God is no less sovereign over the present than he was over the past and will be over the future. (5) And if he is sovereign over the *future*, then the future, too, is not something to be feared, but to be embraced—simply because I belong to Christ, Christ belongs to God, and God controls the future.

So none of these tyrannies—"the world or life or death or the present or the future"—control us any longer. They have been decisively beaten. They are under the sway of the sovereign Redeemer, and since we are the company of the redeemed, they are ours.

There is an exquisite compass of vision here that is tragically lost when all of our Christianity means nothing more than "finding fulfillment" or seeking personal peace or—worse yet—identifying with the "right" party or Christian guru. We are God's, and that transforms everything. If we truly understand this, there are no tyrannies left. We will want all that God has for us, both in this life and in the life to come. And that means we will never reduce the God-sized dimensions of biblical Christianity to all that can be embraced by just one Christian teacher or worker, no matter how able or wise. Factionalism is utter folly. Not only does it hurt the church, it impoverishes all those who embrace it, for it cuts them off from the wealth of the heritage that rightly belongs to all the children of God.

What might this mean for us today, in practical terms? It certainly does not mean that every Christian leader and every Christian heritage has the same worth. In other passages Paul deals with the importance of discernment, of weighing things in order to pursue what is best (e.g., Phil. 1:9–11). Nor does it mean that everything that calls itself "Christian" is necessarily Christian. But it does mean that if you are, say, a Lutheran, you must not cut yourself off from what is right and good in the Wesleyan, Reformed, charismatic, Anabaptist, and other lines. (And of course, I could have rephrased that sentence in any combination.) At the local church level, it will not do to lionize one particular leader (preferably recently retired or deceased!) at the expense of all the others. Ultimately, to do so is to assign him or her almost tyrannical powers. Not only does it breed factionalism, it ignores the vast heritage and wealth that are ours simply because we are Christians and we belong to God. And, in the sense already expressed, what belongs to God belongs to us. Must we have fights over church music? We should have the best, the most God-centered, the most truthful, the most edifying. But must it all be in one style? Is there nothing to be gained from wide exposure to the company of saints in many parts of the world who have expressed their adoration of the Savior with richness of hymnody we can never exhaust, but which we ignore to our detriment?

"All things are yours . . . and you are of Christ, and Christ is of God."

Questions for Review and Reflection

1. According to Paul, who are "carnal" or "worldly" Christians?
2. How does their spiritual immaturity show itself?
3. What two principal truths about Christian leaders do verses 5–17 teach us?
4. Whose works are burned up in verse 15? Articulate the warning in your own words.
5. Explain the last few verses of the chapter in your own words.

4

The Cross and Christian Leadership
1 Corinthians 4

¹So then, men ought to regard us as servants of Christ and as those entrusted with the secret things of God. ²Now it is required that those who have been given a trust must prove faithful. ³I care very little if I am judged by you or by any human court; indeed, I do not even judge myself. ⁴My conscience is clear, but that does not make me innocent. It is the Lord who judges me. ⁵Therefore judge nothing before the appointed time; wait till the Lord comes. He will bring to light what is hidden in darkness and will expose the motives of men's hearts. At that time each will receive his praise from God.

⁶Now, brothers, I have applied these things to myself and Apollos for your benefit, so that you may learn from us the meaning of the saying, "Do not go beyond what is written." Then you will not take pride in one man over against another. ⁷For who makes you different from anyone else? What do you have that you did not receive? And if you did receive it, why do you boast as though you did not?

[8]Already you have all you want! Already you have become rich! You have become kings—and that without us! How I wish that you really had become kings so that we might be kings with you! [9]For it seems to me that God has put us apostles on display at the end of the procession, like men condemned to die in the arena. We have been made a spectacle to the whole universe, to angels as well as to men. [10]We are fools for Christ, but you are so wise in Christ! We are weak, but you are strong! You are honored, we are dishonored! [11]To this very hour we go hungry and thirsty, we are in rags, we are brutally treated, we are homeless. [12]We work hard with our own hands. When we are cursed, we bless; when we are persecuted, we endure it; [13]when we are slandered, we answer kindly. Up to this moment we have become the scum of the earth, the refuse of the world.

[14]I am not writing this to shame you, but to warn you, as my dear children. [15]Even though you have ten thousand guardians in Christ, you do not have many fathers, for in Christ Jesus I became your father through the gospel. [16]Therefore I urge you to imitate me. [17]For this reason I am sending to you Timothy, my son whom I love, who is faithful in the Lord. He will remind you of my way of life in Christ Jesus, which agrees with what I teach everywhere in every church.

[18]Some of you have become arrogant, as if I were not coming to you. [19]But I will come to you very soon, if the Lord is willing, and then I will find out not only how these arrogant people are talking, but what power they have. [20]For the kingdom of God is not a matter of talk but of power. [21]What do you prefer? Shall I come to you with a whip, or in love and with a gentle spirit?

Most people, at some point or other, dream of themselves becoming great leaders. What do their minds conjure up?

It depends a bit, of course, on the field. To be a leader in, say, basketball, does not demand exactly the same gifts as being a leader in the American Needlepoint Guild. Still, there are commonalities. The person who daydreams about being a leader in almost any field imagines what it is like to be the best, or at least to be better than most others—to succeed where others fail, to be stalwart where others stumble, to create where others merely perform, to win adulation and applause, perhaps after some initial hardship and rejection. To be a leader may mean fame, money, and some freedoms from the responsibilities and humdrum existence of ordinary mortals. To be a leader means to win respect. Only rarely do those who dream of leadership, but who have never experienced it, think through the responsibilities, pressures, and temptations leaders face. Almost never do they focus on accountability, service, suffering.

The opening chapters of 1 Corinthians have already introduced us to some elements of Christian leadership, although, of course, this is not the primary theme of the epistle. Throughout 1 Corinthians 1–4 Paul is primarily concerned to address the factionalism that was tearing the church apart with squabbles, jealousy, and one-upmanship. But because not a little of this quarreling arose from the habit of different groups in the church associating themselves with various well-known Christian leaders ("I follow Paul," "I follow Apollos," "I follow Cephas," and so forth; 1:11–12; 3:4), Paul found it necessary to address several Corinthian misconceptions regarding the nature of genuine Christian leadership. These believers were adopting too many models from their surrounding world. They were infatuated with Sophist teachers, many of whom prized form above content, prestige above humility, stoicism above passion, an organizing philosophy ("wisdom") above frank confessions of ignorance and the limitations of human knowledge, rhetoric above truth, money above people, and reputation above integrity. In that sort of environment Paul, as we have discovered, had to return to basics and explain what it means to confess Christ crucified. But he also had to disabuse his readers of the evil in their tendency to lionize certain Christian leaders and ignore others. Thus in 1 Corinthians 3 Paul insists, among other things, that Christian leaders are servants of Christ and are not to be accorded allegiance reserved for God alone. Indeed, as servants, they are accountable to God for the kind of ministry they exercise. Since God cares about his church, he holds its leaders to account. Indeed, he threatens judgment on all who destroy his church.

In 1 Corinthians 4, Paul is still struggling with the factionalism of the Corinthian believers. So when he talks about the nature of Christian leadership, he relates it to the question at hand: "Now, brothers, I have applied these things to myself and Apollos for your benefit . . ." (4:6). Even so, the fact of the matter is that in addressing the Corinthian tendencies toward quarreling and factionalism, Paul here gives us quite a bit of insight as to what it means to be a Christian leader, and it is from this perspective that we shall look at the chapter. Certainly this is not all that the Bible says about the nature of leadership that pleases God, but the principles articulated here are of capital importance. And they are all tied to the cross.

Christian Leadership Means Being Entrusted with the "Mysteries" of God (4:1–7)

Paul begins by telling the Corinthians how they *ought* to think of Christian leaders: "So then, men ought to regard us as servants of Christ and as those entrusted with the secret things of God" (4:1). Two elements stand out, and both are tied to things Paul has already explained. (1) Christian leaders are "servants of Christ." The language is reminiscent of the agricultural analogy in chapter 3 (though the word for "servant" is different). Christian leaders do not try to be independent gurus, all-wise teachers. They see themselves simply as servants and want other Christians to see them that way, too. But they are servants of one particular Master: they serve Jesus Christ. (2) At the heart of the commission they have received from their Master lies one particular assignment. They have been "entrusted with the secret things of God." The expression *secret things* (literally, *mysteries*) is the same one found in 2:7, "God's wisdom *in a mystery*" (NIV, "God's secret wisdom"). You will recall that in the second chapter of this book the nature of the mystery was explored a little. Paul is not saying that the gospel is "mysterious," but that in some ways it was hidden before the coming of Jesus Christ and has now been revealed. The gospel itself is the content of this mystery, God's wisdom summed up under the burden of Paul's preaching: Jesus Christ and him crucified.

There is a sense, of course, in which all Christians are "servants of Christ" and all have been entrusted with the gospel, "the secret things of God." Nevertheless Paul makes it clear that he is still dealing primarily with leaders. He will shortly write, "Now, brothers, I have applied these things to myself and Apollos"— both leaders—"for *your* benefit" (4:6, emphasis added), thus showing that he is still maintaining the distinction between leaders and others that dominates 1 Corinthians 3. It is not that Paul, Apollos, and other leaders are servants of Christ while other Christians are not, nor is it that they are entrusted with the secret things of God while other believers know nothing of them. Leaders are not in a special, priestly class. Rather, what is required in some sense of all believers is peculiarly required of the leaders of believers. There is a difference of degree. That is why Paul will be able to say, "I urge you to imitate me" (4:16).

Those of us who want to be leaders in the church today, then, must begin by recognizing that there is no special, elitist qualification. This observation is entirely in line with the lists of qualifications for leadership given elsewhere in the New Testament. For example, when Paul in 1 Timothy 3:1–7 sets out the qualifications for an overseer ("bishop" in older English), the most remarkable feature of the list is that it is unremarkable. It contains nothing about intelligence, decisiveness, drive, wealth, power. Almost everything on the list is elsewhere in the New Testament required of all believers. For example, the overseer must not be "given to drunkenness" (1 Tim. 3:3)—which certainly does not mean that the rest of us are allowed to get roaring drunk (Eph. 5:18). Overseers must be hospitable (1 Tim. 3:2); but then again, so must all Christians be (Heb. 13:2). The only elements in the list of qualifications for overseers that are not somewhere applied to all Christians are two: (1) "not . . . a recent convert" (1 Tim. 3:6), which certainly cannot be applied to new Christians, and (2) "able to teach" (1 Tim. 3:2), which is bound up with the peculiar ministry responsibilities of the pastor/overseer/elder.

So what we must recognize, both from 1 Timothy 3 and from 1 Corinthians 4, is that the demands of Christian leadership, in the first instance, do not set a Christian apart into exclusive and elitist categories where certain new rules and privileges obtain. Rather, Christian leadership demands a focus of the kinds of characteristics and virtues that ought to be present in Christians everywhere. That is precisely what makes it possible for Christian leaders to serve as models, as well as teachers, in the church of God.

In this context, then, the two elements of Christian leadership that Paul sets out are clear enough. Christian leaders are servants of Christ, and they are entrusted with the gospel, the secret things of God. If all Christians ought to serve Christ, how much more should their leaders do so unambiguously? If all Christians enjoy the secret wisdom imparted by the Spirit, how much more should leaders who have been entrusted with this great heritage handle it wisely?

It is important to think through what these elements mean. In fact, when they are properly understood, they merge into one. The expression rendered "those entrusted with the secret things of God" might more literally be rendered "[household] stewards of the mysteries of God." True, the household steward held a position of trust, but in a society far more hierarchical than ours that position was commonly occupied by servants, even by slaves. The trust that is given them is given to them in their function as servants, as slaves; conversely, when they are called "servants of Christ," the particular obligation laid on them as "servants of Christ" is the obligation to promote the gospel. It is everything that is entailed in being "entrusted with the secret things of God." What it means to be a servant of Christ is to be obligated to promote the gospel by word and example, the gospel of the crucified Messiah.

That is absolutely fundamental. There is no valid Christian leadership that does not throb with this mandate. In the West, we must repent of our endless fascination for "leadership" that smacks much more either of hierarchical models (I am the boss, and, for all below me on the ladder, what I say goes) or of democratic models (give the people what they want; take another survey, conduct another poll, and scratch where they itch). All valid Christian leadership, however varied its style, however wise its use of sociological findings, however diverse its functions, must begin with this fundamental recognition: Christian leaders have been entrusted with the gospel, the secret things of God that have been hidden in ages past but that are now proclaimed, by their ministry, to men and women everywhere. Moreover, they must beware of politely assuming such a stance, while their real interest lies elsewhere. This will not do. The servants of Christ have a fundamental charge laid on them: They have been entrusted with the gospel, and all their service turns on making that gospel known and on encouraging the people of God, by word, example, and discipline, to live it out.

From this fundamental insight into the nature of Christian leadership, Paul might have drawn out many possible corollaries. In fact, he chooses to trace out just two.

Christian leaders must prove faithful to the One who has assigned them their fundamental task (4:1–4). Paul's logic is easy to follow. He has just insisted that Christian leaders are "entrusted with the secret things of God" (4:1). Any thoughtful reader can imagine the entailment: "Now it is required that those who have been given a trust must prove faithful" (4:2). But to whom? Not, ultimately, to the church. Those who are servants of Christ, those who are entrusted with the secret things of God, do not see themselves winning popularity contests—not even within the church's borders. That is what Paul means when he says, "I care very little if I am judged by you or by any human court" (4:3). There is only one Person whose "Well done!" on the last day means anything. In comparison, the approval or disapproval of the church means nothing.

It is not even your own estimate of your service that is important. Feeling good about your ministry may have some limited utility somewhere, but surely it has no ultimate significance. You may think more highly of your service than God does; you may think less of your service than God does. But if you are constantly trying to please yourself, to make self-esteem your ultimate goal, then you are forgetting whose servant you are, whom you must strive to please. So Paul candidly writes, "I do not even judge myself" (4:3). He does not mean that there is no place in his life for self-examination or self-discipline; his own writings contradict any such interpretation (e.g., 1 Cor. 9:24–27; 2 Cor. 13:5). What he means is that his own judging of himself cannot possibly have ultimate significance. As he puts it, "My conscience is clear" (4:4). That is, as he pens these words he is not aware of any sin or failure lurking in his life. Still, he does not know everything, even about himself. However clear his conscience, he could be self-deceived or grossly ignorant. Clear conscience, he writes, "does not make me innocent" (4:4). At the end of the day, there is only one opinion on his service that carries ultimate significance: "It is the Lord who judges me" (4:4).

Paul's first corollary, then, is very simple. Christian leaders worthy of the name will constantly be aware that they owe fealty and devoted allegiance to only one Person: to the Lord who bought them. In derivative ways, of course, it is important for the Lord's servant to try to maintain peace among the Lord's people and to win their confidence and respect. There may be a place for an appropriate letter of commendation (e.g., Phil. 2:19). Still, a leader's ultimate allegiance must not be to the church, or to any individual leader or tradition. It must be to the Lord alone and to the "secret things of God" he has entrusted to him or her. And if that sometimes means there will be a clash of wills between that leader and the church, so be it; the foolishness of Christ crucified must prevail, even when the church as a whole follows some fork in the road that takes it away from the centrality of the gospel. What is far more tragic is the sad spectacle of so-called Christian leaders trying so hard for the approbation of peers and parishioners that their focus is diverted from the gospel and from the "Well done!" of the crucified Messiah.

Those who follow Christian leaders must recognize that leaders are called to please the Lord Christ—and therefore they must refrain from standing in judgment over them (4:5–7). In other words, if it is important for the leaders to see themselves as servants of Christ entrusted with a magnificent commission, it is also important for the rest of the church to see them as ultimately accountable to the Lord Christ, and therefore to avoid judging them as if the church itself were the ultimate arbiter of ministerial success.

It is easy to bleed this passage for more than it actually says. No thoughtful reader can suppose that Paul is abolishing all functions of judgment in the church. After all, in the next chapter of this epistle, he severely reprimands the church for failing to take decisive disciplinary action in a case of immorality (1 Cor. 5). This disciplinary authority of the church extends even to leaders. In the last chapter of 2 Corinthians, Paul clearly expects the believers in Corinth to exercise discipline over the false apostles before he arrives in town and feels constrained to take dramatic action himself. Casual gossip directed against the elders of the church should be ignored, but when critical reports prove true, there is a place for disciplining leaders (1 Tim. 5:19–20). Furthermore, surely no one can imagine that Paul here insists that Christians have no obligation whatsoever to "judge" themselves, to examine and test the reality and consistency of their allegiance to Christ. Although no Christian's opinion of himself or herself has ultimate importance, that does not stop Paul from saying, in the right circumstances, "Examine yourselves to see whether you are in the faith; test yourselves" (2 Cor. 13:5).

If we roam more broadly through the Scriptures, it is easy enough to find passages that prohibit "judging" and then to discover still others that command it. For example, on the one hand we find Jesus saying, "Do not judge, or you too will be judged. For in the same way you judge others, you will be judged, and with the measure you use, it will be measured to you" (Matt. 7:1–2). On the other hand, he says, "Stop judging by mere appearances, and make a right judgment" (John 7:24). This running tension is very strong throughout the New Testament. There is much that condemns what might be called "judgmentalism." At the same time, chapter after chapter exhorts believers to be discerning, to distinguish right from wrong, to pursue what is best, to exercise discipline in the church, and so forth—functions that demand the proper use of judgment.

Getting the balance right in this area has never been easy. Perhaps it is rendered even more difficult today by the onslaught of pluralism. The brand of pluralism I am talking about teaches that all opinions are equally valid, so that the only opinion that is necessarily wrong is the one that says some other opinion is wrong. Applied to religion, no faith is permitted to say that some other faith is wrong; that is viewed as intolerant, bigoted, ignorant. In short, it is not pluralistic. Within this atmosphere, the passages in the Bible that condemn judgmentalism are regularly trotted out as if that is all the Bible has to say on the subject. In many circles today, "Do not judge, or you too will be judged" (Matt. 7:1) has become the best-known verse in the Bible, easily displacing John 3:16. What is regularly forgotten is that a few verses later Jesus tells his disciples, "Do not give dogs what is sacred; do not throw your pearls to pigs" (Matt. 7:6)—which presupposes that somebody has to judge who the dogs and pigs are. In other words, pluralism has invested a tremendous amount of energy and bias in only one side of the biblical presentation.

We may gain some poise and balance if we remember the kinds of people the two sides address. Prohibitions directed against judging have in mind self-righteous people who want to protect their turf. These people are usually fairly legalistic, have all the right answers, desperately want to elevate their "in" group above all others, and are constantly in danger of usurping the place of God. By contrast, biblical injunctions to be discerning or to judge well in some circumstance or other are directed against those who are careless and undisciplined about holy things, especially about the words of God. Such people regularly fly with the crowd rather than thinking through what allegiance to God and his truth entails in some particular cultural context. *It is utterly disastrous to appeal for judgment when forbearance is called for, or to prohibit all judgment when judgment is precisely what is needed.* Both errors seriously damage the church and usually reflect a mind that is unwilling to think its way carefully through the balance and sanity of the Word of God.

So, what was going on in Corinth? It appears that some Corinthian believers were quite prepared to write off certain Christian leaders, simply because they preferred to follow some other leader as a guru. To elevate one leader and offer him or her the allegiance that belongs to God alone is bad enough; to write off all authority in any other Christian leader not only betrays a woeful lack of courtesy, but places the self-appointed judge in the place of God.

Two further considerations ought to temper our tendency to stand in judgment of others. (1) We do not know the end of the story. Some who start well finish poorly; others who start slowly and hesitatingly finish with a flourish of triumph. "Therefore judge nothing before the appointed time; wait till the Lord comes" (4:5a). (2) We do not know the motives of the people we are judging. That is a prerogative preserved for God alone. "He will bring to light what is hidden in darkness and will expose the motives of men's hearts" (4:5b). There are some leaders who function competently and can please great crowds, but whose hearts are seething swamps of lust, arrogance, and ambition. There are others, less gifted perhaps, who struggle quietly and faithfully against major disappointments and pressures, but whose heart cry is, "Here am I. Send me. Make me as holy, as loving, as useful, as a pardoned sinner can be." Should not hidden motivations be taken into account? And who can do so, except God alone?

Perhaps the most remarkable feature of this paragraph of 1 Corinthians is how it ends. With the final day of judgment in view, Paul might have been expected to say, "At that time each will receive his rebuke from God." But instead, he says, "At that time each will receive his praise from God" (4:5c). How wonderful! The King of the universe, the Sovereign who has endured our endless rebellion and sought us out at the cost of his Son's death, climaxes our redemption by praising us! He is a wise Father who knows how to encourage even the feeblest efforts of his children. What this way of concluding the paragraph shows is that in this case, at least, God judges less sternly than the self-appointed judges in the church. Paul here presupposes that the leaders in question are not to be disciplined, shut out, ignored; they are bona fide Christian leaders, and on the last day God himself will praise them.

Of course, this does not mean that everything a Christian leader does is beyond reproach. Barnabas and Peter were less than consistent in Antioch (Gal. 2:11–14); Paul was less than patient with John Mark (Acts 15:37–40); Apollos needed more instruction to correct his preaching (Acts 18:24–28). In every case, some discernment, some judgment by fellow believers was called for. The principle for which Paul is here contending does not entail the conclusion that Christians are to be so wimpy that they make no distinctions whatsoever. Just because Calvinists have important things to learn from Wesley, and Wesleyans from Calvin, does not mean that both men were entirely right in all they said and taught. Paul is not here absolving Christians from the responsibility to discern, to test all teaching by Scripture, to pursue the best. Rather, he is roundly condemning that kind of judging that simply writes a Christian leader off because he does not neatly fit into my camp or because he appears to compete with my preferred guru or because he is not in my pocket.

This will not do. Christian leaders doubtless make all kinds of mistakes and say all kinds of daft things. But they are not pawns the churches are to hire and fire as if they were nothing but the churches' employees. The church is not the head and the pastor the hireling. Both the church and the Christian leader have one supreme head—Jesus Christ himself. Ideally, both the church and the leader should be working in concert under the one Head. In practice, when the church falls away from the gospel, it may be necessary for the leader to take fairly drastic action (as in 2 Cor. 13). When the leader falls away, it is necessary for the church to take action. But both sides must recognize that there is but one Head. And in the Corinthian situation, Paul judges it particularly important for the believers to recognize that Christian leaders are primarily called to serve the Lord Christ; therefore the church does not have the right to stand in judgment over them.

Although Paul has been making his points fairly abstractly, apparently he has been thinking of the explicit factionalism in the Corinthian church. "Now, brothers, I am applying[1] these things to myself and Apollos for your benefit, so that you may learn from us the meaning of the saying, 'Do not go beyond what is written'"(4:6a). Paul's quotation is not a biblical passage. It was probably a common slogan in the early church, akin to "Keep your finger on the text." By elevating criteria of personal taste to the level where they enabled the Corinthians to write some leaders off, the believers in Corinth were not adhering to biblical revelation, but going beyond it. One can as easily distort the truth and balance of Scripture by going beyond it as by denying some parts of it. If on these points the Corinthians will hew closely to the biblical line, they "will not take pride in one man over against another" (4:6).[2] How could they? They will be much more interested in "taking pride" in Christ crucified: "Let him who boasts boast in the Lord" (1:31). One-upmanship among those redeemed by a crucified Messiah is repulsive.

In any case, Paul argues, if you have received some special help or insight or strength at the hand of one particular leader, is

---

1. I think the Greek verb, though aorist, is present-referring (contrast the NIV's "I have applied").
2. First Corinthians 4:6–7 includes some very difficult Greek that could be taken several ways. With some hesitation, I here follow the NIV.

not this one of God's fine gifts to you, rather than a cause for pride? Is this not true of everything we have of any value? Even if we have worked hard, is not the ability to work in large measure the fruit of good health and an upbringing that has bred discipline and responsibility? "For who makes you different from anyone else? What do you have that you did not receive? And if you did receive it, why do you boast as though you did not?" (4:7).

And thus Paul puts his finger on the nub of the problem. This kind of judgmentalism is prompted by pride. The irony is that this disgusting arrogance is being leveled against those who have been entrusted with "the secret things of God," the gospel of the crucified Messiah, the good news by which these judgmental people are saved. How can any thoughtful person be arrogant beside the cross?

Christian Leadership Means Living Life in the Light of the Cross (4:8–13)

Paul's language is now steeped in biting irony. The Corinthians have become smug, self-satisfied, comfortable, proud. "Already you have all you want!"—with the result that they do not hunger for what they do not yet have. "Already you have become rich!"—so they do not seek spiritual wealth or heed Jesus' injunction to lay up treasure in heaven. "You have become kings"—or, better, "You have begun your reign" (cf. NAB, "You have launched upon your reign"). Paul is not talking about the Corinthians' status ("become kings"), but about their perception of their function ("You have begun your reign").

This needs a bit of explanation. From the very beginning, Christians have been taught to look forward to the end of the age, when Christ himself will return. The New Testament closes with the Spirit and the bride (the church) addressing the exalted Lord Jesus and crying, "Come!" (Rev. 22:17). We wait for the consummation of the "salvation that is ready to be revealed in the last time" (1 Pet. 1:5); we are "looking forward to a new heaven and a new earth, the home of righteousness" (2 Pet. 3:13). Nevertheless, Christians rejoice that Jesus Christ has risen from the dead and has already begun his reign. All authority is his in heaven and on earth (Matt. 28:18). We have already been swept into his kingdom. God has "rescued us from the dominion of darkness and brought us into the kingdom of the Son he loves, in whom we have redemption, the forgiveness of sins" (Col. 1:13–14). Paul describes the Spirit of God as the "down payment" and guarantee of the full inheritance still to come.

So in one sense Christians are oriented to the future and are awaiting the kingdom. This stance we may designate *futurist eschatology*. In another sense, Christians have already been transferred out of the kingdom of darkness and into the kingdom of God's Son. We are already in the kingdom. This stance is sometimes referred to as *realized* or *inaugurated eschatology*. And it is very important to get the balance between these two right. If you devote all your energy toward the future, all kinds of warps appear. You might, for instance, follow the example of some believers at Thessalonica, who apparently thought that Jesus' return and the end of the age were so imminent that they could quit their jobs, sponge off those who were still working, and, amidst plenty of enthusiasm, generally begin to act irresponsibly. Alternatively, you may so focus on the future that you unconsciously minimize the great privileges and joys that are already ours in Christ Jesus. In this perception, everything here and now is dark and gloomy and gray, but when the End comes. . . .

On the other hand, you might err the other way and so emphasize the blessings Christians already enjoy that you overlook the fact that some of them are reserved for the future. You start applying to the present passages and themes that congregate around what life will be like after the Messiah comes again. Both Jews who looked forward to the coming of the Messiah and Christians who look forward to his return have insisted that his people will reign with him. The Corinthians, reading this back into the present, felt they had already begun to reign—"and that without us," Paul says somewhat sourly. "How I wish that you really had begun your reign [NIV, had become kings] so that we might have begun to reign with you [NIV, so that we might be kings with you]!" (4:8). That would mean that Christ had returned, that the consummated reign of Christ had begun, and that all Christians were participating in it. But if Christ's consummated kingdom had not yet begun, then the Corinthians were massively mistaken.

Historically, Christians have often messed up the biblical balance in this area by being too wedded to their times and therefore failing to listen carefully and thoughtfully to Scripture. In times of war, famine, or major social disruption, it is not uncommon for untaught Christians to cry, "It is the End!" They don their ascension robes and forget that Jesus told us that no one knows the time or the day or the hour or the season of his return. Alternatively, when things are going reasonably well, when society seems relatively stable, when there is no war on the horizon, when most people in our culture have enough to eat, and when the general mood is hedonistic and success-oriented, untaught Christians adopt their own form of triumphalism. They point out that God is their Father, he is the great King, and therefore (they argue) they should all live as princes and princesses.

Clearly the Corinthians adopted their own form of this over-realized eschatology. It was tied to their pride, their endless one-upmanship. Paul punctured their massive pretensions by assessing the status of the acknowledged leaders of the church, the apostles. "For it seems to me that God has put us apostles on display at the end of the procession, like men condemned to die in the arena" (4:9a). Probably the imagery was drawn from the triumphal processions of returning Roman legions. The senior military people would come first, then the more junior ones. Behind them, the prisoners would be dragged along, in descending order of rank. Among the defeated foes, the lowest classes and the slaves would bring up the rear, eating everyone else's dust, knowing that they were destined for the arena. There they would die at the hands of gladiators or would simply be thrown to the wild beasts for the amusement of the populace. In fact, Paul says, since the stage on which the struggles of the church are being played out takes in the spiritual arena every bit as much as the physical, the apostles "have been made a spectacle to the whole universe, to angels as well as to men" (4:9b).

With stinging irony, Paul draws the contrast out. Alluding to the themes of chapter 1, he writes, "We are fools for Christ, but you are so wise in Christ!" (4:10a). Of course, if they have followed his argument at all, the real fools are the Corinthians themselves—precisely because that is not how they see it. Paul and other spiritual leaders are "fools" only because they have sided with the foolishness of the cross. "We are weak, but you are strong! You are honored, we are dishonored!" (4:10b). The irony is still total. If Paul and his fellow apostles are "weak," it is because they align themselves with the "weakness" of God that is in fact stronger than all human strength. If they are dishonored, they are dishonored by a world that finds the cross foolish, while the only honor the Corinthians have received is self-honor, plus, perhaps, the doubtful plaudits of a world that the believers have formally disavowed by becoming Christians.

Do the Corinthian believers, then, need to get a better glimpse of what true Christian leadership entails? All right, Paul says, here's the picture: "To this very hour we go hungry and thirsty, we are in rags, we are brutally treated, we are homeless. We work hard with our own hands. When we are cursed, we bless; when we are persecuted, we endure it; when we are slandered, we answer kindly. Up to this moment we have become the scum of the earth, the refuse of the world" (4:11–13).

It is not necessary to unpack these shocking lines in detail, but a few comments on them will accentuate their bite. The phrases *to this very hour* and *up to this moment* are probably Paul's way of drawing attention to the eschatological situation. Paul and his fellow apostles are still suffering, up to this moment, even though the eschatological kingdom has been inaugurated by the triumph of Christ. The Corinthians, in other words, are skewing their theology while ignoring the evidence staring them in the face. The deprivation of itinerant ministry ("hungry," "in rags," "brutally treated"), the very stuff of apostolic life, culminates in "we are homeless"—precisely because their "home" is not tied to this world. At first glance, "We work hard with our own hands" is out of place in this list. In fact, because teachers in the Hellenistic world thought manual work beneath them, while Paul frequently supported himself and his team (and sometimes insisted on doing so) through his craft as a leather worker, it was easy for the Corinthians to write him off as an inferior specimen of the teaching profession. But what they despise, he holds up as exemplary. And as for the way to respond to the jibes and taunts of a skeptical world, Paul offers this testimony as a model: "When we are cursed, we bless; when we are persecuted, we endure it; when we are slandered, we answer kindly" (4:12–13)—thus echoing in his own practice the teaching (Luke 6:28) and example (Luke 23:34) of the Lord Jesus himself. To sum it all up, Paul says, he and his fellow apostles "have become the scum of the earth, the refuse of the world" (4:13), everyone's castoffs, everyone's offscourings, everyone's garbage—all that is despised in a society of beautiful and successful people.

Suddenly, we can no longer ignore Paul's model—not the model he himself was for others, that is, but the model he chose for himself. For we are reminded again and again of the cross. The prophet wrote of the suffering Servant, "He had no beauty or majesty to attract us to him, nothing in his appearance that we should desire him. He was despised and rejected by men, a man of sorrows, and familiar with suffering. Like one from whom men hide their faces he was despised and we esteemed him not" (Isa. 53:2b–3). Paul testifies to the Philippians that he wants to experience not only the power of Christ's resurrection, but also the fellowship of sharing in his sufferings (Phil. 3:10). Indeed, elsewhere he writes to the Christians in Rome and tells them that believers are "heirs of God and co-heirs with Christ, if indeed we share in his sufferings in order that we may also share in his glory" (Rom. 8:17). If Paul insists he is a model for others, telling them to imitate him (4:16), it is because he himself follows the example of Christ (11:1).

Paul is not so naive as to think that every Christian should, ideally, suffer the same amount. In fact, in one passage he testifies to his willingness to take on a disproportionate share of sufferings, so that others might be relieved. But what is at stake, for Paul, is a fundamental stance, a way of looking at things. We may summarize it with three points.

We follow a crucified Messiah. All the eschatological promises regarding the new heaven and the new earth, all the blessings of sins forgiven and of the blessed Spirit of God, do not negate the fact that the good news we present focuses on the foolishness of Christ crucified. And that message simply cannot be effectively communicated from the haughty position of the triumphalist's condescension. Until the end of the age, we will take up our cross—that is, we will die to self-interest daily—and follow Jesus. The less any society knows of that way, the more foolish we will seem and the more suffering we will endure. So be it; there is no other way of following Jesus.

Leaders in the church suffer the most. They are not like generals in the military who stay behind the lines. They are the assault troops, the front line people, who lead by example as much as by word. To praise a form of leadership that despises suffering is therefore to deny the faith.

In measure, all Christians are called to this vision of life and discipleship. Paul is about to say, "I urge you to imitate me. For this reason I am sending to you Timothy, my son whom I love, who is faithful in the Lord. He will remind you *of my way of life in Christ Jesus*, which agrees with what I teach everywhere in every church" (4:16–17, emphasis added).

We must frankly recognize that this stance is alien to much of our experience in the Western world. Until fairly recently, even the unconverted in the West largely adhered to Judeo-Christian values. However, that consensus is eroding rapidly, and as it does there will be more and more overt opposition to any form of Christianity that tries to maintain allegiance to the Bible.

But part of the reason why Paul's stance seems alien to many of us is that we have unwittingly become more like Corinthian Christians than like Pauline (that is, biblical!) Christians. Many of us are well-to-do and comfortable, with little incentive to live in vibrant anticipation of Christ's return. Our desire for the approval of the world often outstrips our desire for Jesus' "Well done!" on the last day. The proper place to begin to change this deep betrayal of the gospel is at the cross—in repentance, contrition, and renewed passion not only to make the gospel of the crucified Messiah central in all our preaching and teaching, but in our lives and the lives of our leaders as well.

Christian Leadership Means Encouraging— and If Necessary, Enforcing—the Way of the Cross Among the People of God (4:14–21)

It is not enough for a Christian leader to have many people following. After all, this leader may be building with sloppy materials and inferior workmanship (3:12–15). The Christian leader must not only preach the message of the cross and live life in the light of the cross, but must foster genuinely Christian living. Mere orthodoxy is not enough; Christians must live out their creed. The gospel of the crucified Messiah must transform not only our beliefs but our behavior. And where deviations from the way of the cross are sufficiently notorious, that leader may have to resort to some form of discipline.

Encouraging the Believers (4:14–17)

Paul begins with the gentler alternative. Despite the biting irony he has just deployed in the previous paragraph, Paul now insists, "I am not writing this to shame you, but to warn you, as my dear children" (4:14). At one level, of course, he certainly is shaming them. But that is not the reason he writes as he does. He writes, rather, to "warn" them—or, more accurately translated, to "admonish" them, to correct them, to encourage them in the right way. On some points that Paul will later bring up, the Corinthian behavior is so shocking that Paul then does openly try to shame them (6:1–6; 15:34); but not here.

Still using the gentle touch, Paul reminds them that he is the one who led them to the Lord in the first place. He casts his appeal in terms of a comfortable, first-century family. With understandable hyperbole, Paul tells the Corinthians that even if they had "ten thousand guardians in Christ" they have only one father. The guardian in the first-century Hellenistic household was usually a trusted slave who was put in charge of the child, bringing the child (usually a son) to and from school and generally supervising his conduct. Such guardians exercised a certain authority over the child, of course, but it would never equal that of the father. Paul was the one who first brought the gospel to the Corinthians; in that sense, he alone became their "father," a fact nothing could change. Paul is careful, of course, not to give the impression that he himself effected their conversion, almost as if he had some magical power. Far from it; he became their father "through the gospel" (4:15). He preached the gospel to them. In God's grace, the gospel transformed them, for it is the gospel that is "the power of God for the salvation of everyone who believes" (Rom. 1:16). Even so, his relationship with the Corinthians is something that can never be duplicated or displaced. Paul sowed the seed; others watered it. Paul laid the foundation; others built on it. Paul "sired" the Corinthian believers through the gospel; others have served as guardians.

"Therefore," Paul writes, "I urge you to imitate me" (1 Cor. 4:16). The logic implied by the *therefore* may escape the modern reader, for in our families there is no pressure for the son to imitate his father. In fact, many of us are such rugged individualists that we often sport our independence as a badge of honor. But in the first century—indeed, in virtually every preindustrial culture—sons were expected to "imitate" their fathers. Vocationally, if the father was a baker, the son would likely become a baker; if the father was a sheep farmer, that is what the son would almost certainly become. The son was expected to carry on family values, family heritage, the family name. With that cultural expectation controlling his analogy, Paul argues that if he became the "father" of the Corinthians, therefore they ought to imitate him.

In the context of these chapters, of course, what Paul wants them to imitate is his passion to live life in the light of the cross. He does not expect them to suffer in exactly the same way he does; he does not demand that they all become apostles or plant churches in distant lands. What he does expect of them is that they will imitate his values, his stance with respect to the world, his priorities, and his valuation of the exclusive centrality of the gospel of the crucified Messiah.

Paul cannot say everything in a letter. So he resolves to send Timothy, "my son whom I love, who is faithful in the Lord." Doubtless, Paul commends Timothy so heartily because he wants the Corinthians to receive him and treat him warmly. Paul tells the Corinthians exactly why he is sending his younger colleague: "He will remind you of my way of life in Christ Jesus, which agrees with what I teach everywhere in every church" (4:17).

There are two stunning elements in this commission. First, Paul is not sending Timothy simply to lay out doctrine, but to remind the Corinthians of Paul's "way of life in Christ Jesus." Biblical Christianity embraces both creed and conduct, both belief and behavior. Sometimes the elementary truths of Scripture are not understood or believed, and it is necessary to go over the basics again. Here, however, Paul gives the impression that the biggest problem with the Corinthians is that they are not living up to what they know. Judging by these first four chapters of his epistles to them, many of the Corinthians were not even making the connections between what they believed and how they should live. They would be the first to insist that Jesus died for their sins and rose again, but they could not grasp how this historical reality, this supreme moment in God's redemptive purposes, not only achieved their salvation but must shape the way they live. So Paul sends Timothy to remind his readers of his "way of life"—a way of life that agrees with what Paul teaches.

This suggests that the Christian leader today not only must teach the gospel, but also must teach how the gospel works out in daily life and conduct. And that union must be modeled as well as explained.

This is a vision of what Christian leadership must try to do that we badly need to recapture. The need is evident even at a confessional seminary like the one at which I teach. Increasingly, we have students who come from thoroughly pagan or secular backgrounds, who have been converted in their late teens or twenties, and who come to us in their thirties. Not uncommonly, they spring from dysfunctional families, and they carry a fair bit of baggage. More dramatically yet, a surprising number of them cannot easily make connections between the truths of the gospel and how to live.

A couple of years ago a student who was about to graduate was called in by one of our faculty members who had learned the student was planning to return to computer science and abandon plans to enter vocational ministry. The student was pleasant, with a solid B+ to his credit. But as the faculty member probed, it became obvious that this student had not put it all together. He could define propitiation but did not know what it was like to feel forgiven. He could defend the priority of grace in salvation but still felt as if he could never be good enough to be a minister. He could define holiness but found himself practicing firm self-discipline rather than pursuing holiness. His life and his theological grasp had not come together.

Mercifully, this particular faculty member was spiritually insightful. He took the student back to the cross and worked outward from that point. The student began to weep and weep as he glimpsed the love of God for him. Today he is in the ministry.

Faithful Christian leaders must make the connections between creed and conduct, between the cross and how to live. And they must exemplify this union in their own lives.

In the second element of Paul's two-part commission to Timothy, he says that what Timothy will convey agrees with what he teaches "everywhere in every church" (4:17). In 1 Corinthians Paul repeatedly makes the same point: he is consistent in his teaching and life, and expects the same substance to be lived out in every church (see 7:17; 11:16; 14:33). This suggests that the Corinthian church was constantly trying to prove how independent it was. Paul is saying that there is a kind of creativity that takes one outside the orb of faithful Christianity everywhere.

Warning the Believers (4:18–21)

Paul is the first to recognize that not every problem will be cleared up with one letter. In this case, the sad state of affairs in the Corinthian church is traceable to a segment of the church that Paul labels "arrogant." In most institutions, a relatively small number of people largely shapes the opinions of virtually the entire body. In this case, these arrogant, self-appointed opinion-makers had not only swayed the congregation, but were openly banking on Paul's absence: "Some of you have become arrogant, as if I were not coming to you" (4:18). Paul cannot give a definite time when he will show up, but he promises to come "very soon, if the Lord is willing" (4:19). He recognizes, with James, that plans for the future must always be subject to "If it is the Lord's will" (James 4:15–16). When Paul comes, he will "find out not only how these arrogant people are talking, but what power they have. For the kingdom of God is not a matter of talk but of power" (4:19–20).

To understand this threat, it is important, once more, to remember the flow of the argument. What Paul says, literally, is that he will find out "not the word of these arrogant people, but the power." Immediately we are reminded of the discussion in 1 Corinthians 1. The Corinthians had become intoxicated by the "wisdom of word," but were thereby emptying the cross of Christ of its power (1:17). They were so enamored of form and rhetoric that showing off with eloquence became more important to them than the gospel, which is displayed in its greatest power when it is not running noisy competition with people more interested in promoting themselves than in God's power (2:1–5). When Paul comes, however, he will not be impressed by their "word"; he won't really care "how these arrogant people are talking," no matter how eloquent their rhetoric. No, he will be interested in only one thing: What power do they have? In the light of 1:18–2:5, this is the power of the gospel, the power to forgive, to transform, to call men and women out of darkness and into the kingdom of God's dear Son. Mere talk will not change people; the gospel will. So Paul is going to ask for their credentials: What people has your eloquence genuinely transformed by bringing them into a personal knowledge of the crucified Messiah? He is going to expose them for the empty, religious windbags that they are.

It is possible that Paul's threat goes deeper yet. At the beginning of the next chapter he deals directly with a man whose sexual sin cries out to be confronted by the discipline of the church. He expects the church to hand this man over to Satan (5:5). But there is evidence elsewhere that where the church is unwilling to exercise this sort of discipline, Paul will take action by himself. In Ephesus, for instance, were two men who had "shipwrecked their faith," Hymenaeus and Alexander by name, "whom," Paul writes, "I have handed over to Satan to be taught not to blaspheme" (1 Tim. 1:20). In a later epistle to the Corinthians Paul warns that he might have to be "harsh" in his use of his apostolic authority, if they do not get their house in order (2 Cor. 13:10).

In other words, bringing the people of God to consistent Christian living in the light of the gospel of the crucified Messiah is so important to Paul that he will not turn from this goal. If he moves people in this direction by encouragement and admonition, all to the good; if severer discipline is called for, he will not flinch. So Paul offers the Corinthians a choice: "What do you prefer? Shall I come to you with a whip, or in love and with a gentle spirit?" (4:21). He does not mean, of course, that if he comes with a whip (literally, a "rod" of correction, continuing the father/son metaphor) he will not love them. The contrast refers to the manner or form of his coming, not his motives. But spankings still hurt, even from a father who insists that he is spanking his son because he loves him. It is much better for the son to change his behavior, so that the manner of the father's coming will be not with discipline but with a gentle spirit.

In short, Christian leaders dare not overlook their responsibility to lead the people of God in living that is in conformity with the gospel. That is why Paul urges people to live a life worthy of the calling they have received (Eph. 4:1). It is why Paul prays that believers may live a life worthy of the Lord, the crucified Messiah, and may please him in every way (Col. 1:10). And if the people of God dig in their heels in disobedience, there may come a time for Christian leaders to admonish, to rebuke, and ultimately to discipline firmly those who take the name of Christ but do not care to follow him. The sterner steps must never be taken hastily or lightly. But sometimes they must be taken. That is part of the responsibility of Christian leadership.

Questions for Review and Reflection

1. What does it mean to be "entrusted with the secret things of God"?
2. When should Christians "judge" others? When should they stop themselves from judging others?
3. What examples of being a "spectacle" for Christ's sake have you heard about or experienced?
4. How does Paul intend to bring together in his converts the gospel as a creed and genuine Christian living?
5. How should Christian leadership differ from most leadership in the broader world?

5

The Cross and the World Christian
1 Corinthians 9:19–27

[19]Though I am free and belong to no man, I make myself a slave to everyone, to win as many as possible. [20]To the Jews I became like a Jew, to win the Jews. To those under the law I became like one under the law (though I myself am not under the law), so as to win those under the law. [21]To those not having the law I became like one not having the law (though I am not free from God's law but am under Christ's law), so as to win those not having the law. [22]To the weak I became weak, to win the weak. I have become all things to all men so that by all possible means I might save some. [23]I do all this for the sake of the gospel, that I may share in its blessings.

[24]Do you not know that in a race all the runners run, but only one gets the prize? Run in such a way as to get the prize. [25]Everyone who competes in the games goes into strict training. They do it to get a crown that will not last; but we do it to get a crown that will last forever. [26]Therefore I do not run like a

man running aimlessly; I do not fight like a man beating the air. [27]No, I beat my body and make it my slave so that after I have preached to others, I myself will not be disqualified for the prize.

I had better begin by explaining what I mean by a "world Christian."

I am certainly not referring to "worldly" Christians (3:1–4). We spent enough time on them in the third chapter of this book. By contrast, the expression *world Christian* has taken on quite a different and specialized meaning among missionaries and others, owing in part to the increasing globalization (another newly coined word!) of the church. *Globalization* is a term that includes a brace of related phenomena. Missionaries are no longer going in only one direction, from the so-called First World to the so-called Third World, but are moving from many parts of the world to many other parts. Communications facilities are enabling believers all over the world to work together on concrete projects and forms of outreach. Increasingly, the church in any one part of the world is pulled into the orbit of what takes place in many other parts of the world. Theological reflection and patterns of biblical and theological training are no longer exclusively tied to the models created in the West and exported to other parts of the globe. Global movements of money and personnel change many priorities—both within the church and outside it.

Almost in reaction against such globalization, many people are responding with increasing nationalism, sometimes with almost frightening ethnocentrism. Christians are not immune to these sweeping currents of thought. They, too, can be caught up in flag-waving nationalism that puts the interests of my nation or my class or my race or my tribe or my heritage above the demands of the kingdom of God. Instead of feeling that their most important citizenship is in heaven, and that they are just passing through down here on their way "home" to the heavenly Jerusalem (Heb. 12:22–23), they become embroiled with petty priorities that constitute an implicit denial of the lordship of Christ.

What we need, then, are world Christians—not simply American Christians or British Christians or Kenyan Christians, but world Christians. By "world Christians," I am referring to Christians, genuine believers in the Lord Jesus Christ, of whom the following things are true:

> Their allegiance to Jesus Christ and his kingdom is self-consciously set above all national, cultural, linguistic, and racial allegiances.
>
> Their commitment to the church, Jesus' messianic community, is to the church everywhere, wherever the church is truly manifest, and not only to its manifestation on home turf.
>
> They see themselves first and foremost as citizens of the heavenly kingdom and therefore consider all other citizenship a secondary matter.
>
> As a result, they are single-minded and sacrificial when it comes to the paramount mandate to evangelize and make disciples.

The church, of course, is the only institution with eternal significance. If anyone ought to transcend the limitations of merely temporal allegiances, then those who constitute the church should.

In the passage before us, Paul, the quintessential world Christian, lays out a number of convictions and priorities that we must adopt if we are to be world Christians ourselves.

We Must Know What Freedoms and Constraints Are Ours in Jesus Christ

Paul opens with what appears on first reading to be a straightforward contradiction. He is talking about how he flexes what we would today call his lifestyle as he attempts to evangelize different groups of people. "To the Jews I became like a Jew, to win the Jews" (9:20a). Then he explains what characteristic it is in the Jews that demands genuine flexibility on his part: "To those under the law I became like one under the law (*though I myself am not under the law*), so as to win those under the law" (9:20b, emphasis added). On the other hand, Paul behaved rather differently among the Gentiles: "To those not having the law I became like one not having the law (*though I am not free from God's law but am under Christ's law*), so as to win those not having the law" (9:21, emphasis added). So is Paul under the law, or not?

The meaning of the passage is much disputed. I shall try to circle in on it by a number of steps.

1. It is clear that Paul sees himself in what might be called a third position. He does not see himself as a Christian Jew, someone who normally obeys the Mosaic law and who has to flex in order to win Gentiles.[1] Nor does he see himself as a Gentile, someone who has to take on the burden of the law afresh in order to win the Jews. He sees himself, rather, in a third position, from which he has to flex to win Jews on the one hand and Gentiles on the other. "To those under the law I *became* like one under the law. . . . To those not having the law I *became* like one not having the law" (emphasis added). Paul occupies a third position.

2. When Paul says that he bends to "become" like a Jew or to "become" like a Gentile, he immediately introduces a parenthetical remark that establishes the limitations on his flexibility. It is these parenthetical remarks that are so difficult. On the one hand, to those under the law he becomes like one under the law—which presumably means he scrupulously observes kosher laws and other points that would enable him to move freely in the Jewish communities and gain a hearing—even though, he parenthetically insists, he is not himself under the law. On the other hand, to those without the law he becomes like one not having the law—which presumably means he ignores the legal constraints that set Jews off from Gentiles and lives freely among the Gentiles as one of them—even though, he parenthetically insists, he is not free to do anything whatsoever; he is not free from "God's law" but is "under Christ's law." Unless Paul is simply contradicting himself, he cannot mean by "God's law" in the second case exactly what he means by "the law" in the first.

Still, whatever he means by saying he is not free from God's law, there is something intuitively obvious about it. We can easily

---

1. In some contexts, of course, that is precisely how Paul thinks of himself: a Christian Jew. That is the self-identification that makes his anguish in Romans 9:1–5 so poignant. Elsewhere he reminds his readers that he sprang from the tribe of Benjamin (Phil. 3:5). Such passages serve to make 1 Corinthians 9 the more striking. In this context, where he talks about his relation to the law, Paul does not identify himself as a Christian Jew or a Christian Gentile, but as something else.

hear Paul saying, "To the Jew I became a Jew," and "To the Gentile I became a Gentile"; we cannot imagine him saying, "To the gossip I became a gossip," and "To the adulterer I became an adulterer." In other words, while saying he is not under the law as other Jews were, he certainly does not mean to suggest he is an utter antinomian (someone who feels completely free from all of God's demands and commands).

3. There are other passages, even within 1 Corinthians, where God's "law" or God's "commands" cannot be reduced to the Mosaic code. The most discussed, I imagine, is 1 Corinthians 7:19: "Circumcision is nothing and uncircumcision is nothing. Keeping God's commands is what counts." Some Christians who make much of the law love to cite the second part of this verse, "Keeping God's commands is what counts." What has to be remembered, of course, is that the average first-century Jew would have said, "Wait a minute! Circumcision *is* one of God's commands. How can you say that circumcision is nothing, and then immediately comment, 'Keeping God's commands is what counts'?" The only answer is that, for Paul, the commands of God that he finds operative for the Christian cannot be equated with the Mosaic code.

4. If I understand 1 Corinthians 9:19–23 correctly, what Paul says is that he is not under the (Mosaic) law-covenant (a common meaning of *nomos*, the NIV's "law"). It is no longer the law-covenant that binds him to the God of his fathers. In order to win his fellow Jews, he is happy to live under the stipulations of that law-covenant and not be unnecessarily offensive to them, but he insists that the law-covenant no longer binds him. It cannot; he is under a new covenant (cf. 1 Cor. 11:25). On the other side, to win those not having the law of God expressed in the old covenant—namely, Gentiles—he is prepared to live like those without any of the constraints of the law-covenant upon them; but there are constraints beyond which he cannot go. He is not infinitely flexible; he is not "free from God's law." This cannot mean he is not free from the (Mosaic) law-covenant, for he has just said he is. Rather, he means, I think, that he is not free from God's demands, God's requirements. And then he stipulates exactly where those requirements lie: "I am not free from God's law," he writes, *"but am under Christ's law"* (emphasis added). The expres-

sion is a peculiar one, but the heart of the idea is clear enough. All of God's demand upon him is mediated through Christ. Whatever God demands of him as a new-covenant believer, a Christian, binds him; he cannot step outside those constraints. There is a rigid limit to his flexibility as he seeks to win the lost from different cultural and religious groups: he must not do anything that is forbidden to the Christian, and he must do everything mandated of the Christian. He is not free from God's law; he is under Christ's law.

Thus, although this passage is sometimes interpreted to mean that we should feel free to reshape the gospel when we move from culture to culture, that is exactly what Paul does *not* mean. Paul is prepared to be extraordinarily flexible wherever the law of God, mediated through Christ, does not impinge on him. But he himself is under "Christ's law," which in this epistle is clearly bound up with the gospel itself, the gospel of the crucified Messiah.

5. The obvious question, at this point, is how Christ's law, which Paul says binds him, is related to the Mosaic law-covenant, which Paul says does not bind him. It is one thing for Paul to say he is not under covenant A but under covenant B. It would be quite another thing to say that the commands and the prohibitions of the two covenants are completely disjunctive, so that they have nothing in common. They cannot be *precisely* the same in their commands, or it is difficult to see how one could speak of two covenants. But granted the God of the Bible, it is unthinkable to suppose that the two covenants are completely disjunctive in their respective commands. So that raises the legitimate question, How are the commands, the "laws" in the modern sense of that word, of the new covenant related to the commands, the "laws," of the old?

Although that question is important and has a long and tangled history of interpretation, I am not going to broach it here, as it would take us too far away from the point toward which I am moving. At that point Paul will not budge.

6. The purpose of this rather complex discussion should now be clear. Although Paul was an extraordinarily flexible apostle and evangelist, he had sorted through elemental Christianity in a profound and nuanced way so that he knew when he could be flexible and when he should not bend. In other words, his grasp

of theology enabled him to know who he was, what was expected of him, what he was free to do, and what he should not consider doing under any circumstances.

In short, we must also know what freedoms and constraints are ours in Jesus Christ. The *only* way to achieve this maturity is to think through Scripture again and again to try to grasp the system of its thought—how the parts cohere and combine to make sense.

Of course, this is not the only passage that is very important to help Christians come to grips with who they are. There are many, many others. Christians are those who have been justified by faith in Christ Jesus and, in consequence, have peace with God (Rom. 5:1). Christians are those who call on the name of the Lord Jesus Christ (1 Cor. 1:2). Christians are those who pray that the power of God may so rest on them that Christ dwells in their hearts through faith, while they themselves increasingly grasp the limitless dimensions of God's love for them in Christ Jesus (Eph. 3:14–21). It is immensely important that Christians know who they are as children of the living God, what is expected of them, where they may be flexible, and where they must be as rigid as tensile steel.

It is only the person who gains this knowledge who can join Paul in saying, without compromise, "I have become all things to all men" (9:22). Today that expression, "all things to all men," is often used as a form of derision. He (or she) has no backbone, we say; he is two-faced; he is "all things to all men." But Paul wears the label as a witness to his evangelistic commitment. Even so, he could not do this if he did not know who he was as a Christian. The person who lives by endless rules and who forms his or her self-identity by conforming to them simply cannot flex at all. By contrast, the person without roots, heritage, self-identity, and nonnegotiable values is not really flexing, but is simply being driven hither and yon by the vagaries of every whimsical opinion that passes by. Such people may "fit in," but they cannot win anyone. They hold to nothing stable or solid enough to win others to it! Thus the end of Paul's statement in verse 22 is critical: "I have become all things to all men *so that by all possible means I might save some*" (9:22, emphasis added). This perspective is so important that I shall return to it.

When in the last century Hudson Taylor, the founder of the China Inland Mission (now the Overseas Missionary Fellowship), started to wear his hair long and braided like Chinese men of the time and to put on their clothes and to eat their food, many of his fellow missionaries derided him. But Hudson Taylor had thought through what was essential to the gospel (and was therefore nonnegotiable) and what was a cultural form that was neither here nor there, and might in fact be an unnecessary barrier to the effective proclamation of the gospel.

To be a world Christian, then, it is important to grow in your grasp of Scripture and in your exposure to other cultures, so that you do not tie your cultural preferences to the gospel and invest the former with the authority of the latter. This is not to say that all cultural elements are morally neutral. Far from it. *Every* culture has good and bad elements in it. Wicked people can manipulate the appeal to culture to persecute Christians (as is done, for instance, in Acts 16:20–21). Yet in every culture it is important for the evangelist, church planter, and witnessing Christian to flex as far as possible, so that the gospel will not be made to appear unnecessarily alien at the merely cultural level. But it is also important to recognize evil elements in culture when they appear and to understand how biblical norms assess them. There will be times when it is necessary to confront culture. After all, simply to appeal to current cultural norms, all the while demanding more flexibility from the Christian, is simply a way of saying that the gospel does not have the right to stand in judgment over culture—and that will not do.

Even to begin to assess such matters aright, we must know what freedoms and constraints are ours in Christ Jesus. We must develop a firm grasp of biblical theology.

We Must Not Stand On Our "Rights"

This part of Paul's argument becomes very clear if we trace his thought from 1 Corinthians 8:1 to 11:1, a passage that hangs together as a unit controlled by two or three themes. We cannot pause now to follow the fine points of his argument, but there are some elements of it that can be quickly summarized and that neatly establish the point: we must not stand on our "rights."

First Corinthians 8 is largely given over to a discussion of whether or not Christians should eat meat that has been offered to idols. It appears that most meat was butchered in connection with a temple guild and sold just outside the temple doors. Christians recently converted out of raw paganism tended to think that the purchase and eating of such meat was a dangerous compromise. It flagged an interest in the old pagan gods, and therefore involved the Christian in idolatry. Other Christians, more mature, felt that slapping a piece of meat down in front of a stone idol did not affect the meat; it was still meat, nothing more, and could be purchased and eaten with a clear conscience. Just because the pagans thought the idol represented a god did not mean that Christians had to indulge in such superstitions. And so the Corinthian church was divided.

Paul's handling of the matter is instructive. In the tenth chapter of his epistle, he absolutely prohibits any involvement in the worship conducted in the pagan temple. Behind the idols are demonic forces too dangerous to play with. Besides, you cannot participate in cultic rituals without aligning yourself with the fellowship of idol worshipers. Stay away!

Back in chapter 8, however, Paul's line of thought is more nuanced. On the one hand, he agrees that buying meat that had been slaughtered in front of an idol is no compromise in and of itself. The meat is not affected. On the other hand, those who think this *is* a compromise and whose consciences Paul labels "weak" (because they think something is evil that is not really evil) should not buy and eat such meat. They would be wounding their weak consciences. Paul judges it dangerous for Christians to defy their consciences, because if they get in the habit of ignoring the voice of conscience, they may ignore that voice *even when the conscience is well informed and is warning them off something that is positively evil.* Doubtless, on the long haul Paul would like these weak Christians to grow in their knowledge of the Scriptures and the gospel so that they will not think something is evil that is not (like eating meat that had been offered to idols); but until they have reached such maturity, they must not defy their own consciences.

Meanwhile, Paul tells those with "strong" consciences (strong because they are sufficiently informed that on this issue at least they do not label anything evil that is not really evil) that they are right on the issue of meat offered to idols, but that the discussion must not end there. They should also feel an obligation toward their "weaker" brothers and sisters in Christ. If those with a weak conscience should spot another, older, allegedly wiser, believer eating meat that had been offered to idols, they might be emboldened to do the same thing—in defiance of their own consciences and therefore to their own spiritual detriment. For the strong believers to insist on their rights would be heartless. "When you sin against your brothers in this way and wound their weak conscience, you sin against Christ. Therefore, if what I eat causes my brother to fall into sin, I will never eat meat again, so that I will not cause him to fall" (8:12–13).

There are two elements in this spiritual counsel that must be understood.

First, the kind of situation Paul is facing here must not be confused with quite a different one. Suppose you are a Christian who, owing to your cultural background, has always engaged in social drinking. Now you move into a circle that is more socially conservative. Some senior saint comes up to you and says, "I have to tell you that I am offended by your drinking. Paul tells us that if anyone is offended by what you do, you must stop it. I'm offended; you must therefore stop your drinking." How would you respond?

This senior saint is simply manipulating you. He (or she) is not a person with a weak conscience who is in danger of tippling on the side because of your example, and thus wounding his weak conscience. Far from it. If he sees you drinking again he will likely denounce you in the most unrestrained terms. In his eyes, he is the stronger person, not the weaker. In other words, this case is not at all like the one the apostle had to deal with. Indeed, it might be wise to tell him, "I'm sorry to hear that you have such a weak conscience." He will probably be so unclear as to what you mean that he may actually leave you alone for a couple of weeks. To develop a modern example somewhat akin to what Paul faces, we would have to change the story somewhat. Now you have become a youth sponsor in a church. Some of the young people from socially conservative homes see you drinking and, against the conscience they have developed over such matters, follow suit; in time they become sloppy about all kinds of serious moral issues. You have thus become party to their substantial destruction.

The point to observe is that in Paul's case the believer with the strong conscience is not manipulated into conformity by a bludgeoning from a senior saint who wants everyone to obey the same rules. Rather, the strong believer is exhorted to give up his rights for the sake of others. The appeal, finally, is love for brothers and sisters in Christ. Strong Christians may be right on a theological issue, but unless they voluntarily abandon what is in fact their right they will do damage to the church and thus "sin against Christ" (8:12). To stand on your rights may thus involve you in sin after all—not the sin connected with your rights (there, after all, you are right!), but the sin of lovelessness, the sin of being unwilling to forgo your rights for the spiritual and eternal good of others. How can Christians stand beside the cross and insist on their rights?

Second, Paul cannot be written off as an utterly dispassionate and merely academic theologian. He dares offer himself as an example of what strong Christians should imitate: "Therefore, if what I eat causes my brother to fall into sin, I will never eat meat again, so that I will not cause him to fall" (8:13).

This verse serves as a transition to 1 Corinthians 9, which Paul devotes to explaining his own motives and self-discipline. In fact, Paul is accomplishing two things in this chapter. On the one hand, he is simply showing on how many fronts he practices what he preaches: in addition to other things, he cheerfully gives up his rights for the spiritual good of others. At the same time, it seems clear that at least some in the Corinthian church did not hold him in very high regard, precisely because in their view he did not stand up for himself. He did not throw his authority around and make people respect him. They were so attuned to the forms of leadership in first-century pagan Corinth, especially those of the sophists and other traveling teachers, that they simply did not understand a preacher like Paul. In part, therefore, Paul is here offering a defense of his priorities: "This is my defense to those who sit in judgment on me" (9:3). What Paul provides us with is a deeply Christian explanation of his principled self-denial.

Paul begins his defense by insisting that he is an apostle. He
saw the risen Lord and received his commission directly from
him. In a gentle dig, Paul suggests that even if others find
grounds to doubt the legitimacy of his apostleship, the Corinthians themselves have little excuse. They exist as Christians
because they are the fruit of his apostolic ministry (9:1–2)!

The nub of the charge against Paul, it appears, is that he
refuses support ("the right to food and drink," 9:4) from the
Corinthians and that he does not travel in his itinerant ministry
with the kinds of comfort and support that senior leaders should
expect—such as bringing along a spouse on an expense-paid trip.
It may be hard for us at first to understand why this should be
thought so serious a charge. But in much of the first-century Hellenistic world, traveling teachers were assessed, in part, by the
amount of money they could take in. People wanted to brag
about how much money they had paid to Professor So-and-so for
a course of lectures—just as there are some people today who
boast, in a complaining sort of way, about how much it is costing
them to send their son or daughter to Harvard. If Paul would not
accept money from the Corinthians, who wanted to lavish it on
him so they could feel good about how important their guru was,
many felt it proved he did not really understand the rules of the
game, and so he could not amount to much. From the Corinthian
perspective, Paul denigrated himself yet further by doing manual
labor—something no respectable Hellenistic teacher would have
dreamed of doing! The problem of the Corinthian attitude
toward money and teaching surfaces even more poignantly in
2 Corinthians 11:7ff.[2]

Paul begins to address this problem by insisting that he has the
right to support. It is silly to imagine that only he and Barnabas
have to work for a living (9:6). Soldiers serve and are paid by
those whom they serve; vinedressers and shepherds are supported out of the profits gained from their toil. Should we not

2. Paul's approach to support from the churches he founded is complex and cannot be fully probed here. It is quite certain that he did sometimes accept money
from churches he founded, notably the Philippian church. It appears, however,
that he never accepted money from them for services rendered. That is, he was
not "paid" for ministry in, say, Philippi, but he would accept money from Philippi when he was serving in Corinth. There were several other subtle principles
that governed his fiscal decisions as well.

expect those who teach the Word to be supported out of the fruit of their toil—the converts they have won (9:7)? Scripture itself gives ample precedent for the principle that workers—animals or people—should be supported out of their labor (9:8–10). If Paul has sown "spiritual seed" among the Corinthians, surely it is not too much to expect that he would reap a "material harvest" from them (9:11)! And after all, the Corinthian believers have supported other Christian leaders. Does not Paul have the right to expect the same (9:12a)?

Then the punch line: "But we did not use this right. On the contrary, we put up with anything rather than hinder the gospel of Christ" (9:12b). From Paul's perspective, accepting money from these people while he was planting a church among them might prove detrimental to the integrity of his witness and the credibility of the gospel, so he voluntarily gave up his right to support. This does not mean that he thinks all Christian leaders, or all church planters, ought to adopt the same policy. Far from it. He insists that in the normal way of things those who work in the religious arena should be supported out of the fruit of their work; "those who preach the gospel should receive their living from the gospel" (9:13–14). Then the point: "But I have not used any of these rights" (9:15). Nor is Paul now stooping to a tactic used in some missionary prayer letters, where by protesting how they do not ask, the writers are in fact asking! Not so with Paul, for he adds, "And I am not writing this in the hope that you will do such things for me. I would rather die than have anyone deprive me of this boast [that is, that he has abandoned the right to be supported by those to whom he ministers]" (9:15).

This seems at first to be rather extreme, even shocking, language. But in a few lines that are often misunderstood, Paul explains why he adopts this stance. In his case, he says, he really has no choice as to whether he will preach the gospel. The other apostles were in some sense volunteers. At least two or three of them sought Jesus out while they were still disciples of John the Baptist (John 1:35–41). All of them were invited by Jesus to join his band and grew in their understanding and faith throughout Jesus' ministry, crowning their ups and downs with the conviction that became theirs in the wake of the resurrection and Pentecost. Not so Paul. The resurrected Jesus appeared to him in brilliant light on the Damascus road and effected his salvation and his call to ministry in one searing revelation. Paul cannot abandon his preaching without abandoning his salvation; to him, the two are of a piece. Thus Paul never volunteered. He was simply captured by Christ for salvation and apostolic ministry in one blinding act of self-disclosure by the glorified Christ. Others may have been volunteers. "Yet when I preach the gospel, I cannot boast, for I am compelled to preach. Woe to me if I do not preach the gospel! If I preach voluntarily, I have a reward; if not voluntarily, I am simply discharging the trust committed to me" (9:16–17). In other words, although many preachers feel some form of divine compulsion, Paul's sense of divine compulsion is unique. It is bound up with the uniqueness of his conversion.

"What then is my reward?" Paul asks (9:18). If his preaching does not prove his wholehearted, voluntary commitment to the task (since he really has no choice in the matter, short of trying to walk away from the gospel altogether), how can he show that his heart and soul are in this ministry? What element in his ministry proves that the grace of God has captured his heart and will, and that his actions bring the rewards of God with them? "Just this: that in preaching the gospel I may offer it free of charge, and so not make use of my rights in preaching it" (9:18).

This is staggering. Paul is so concerned to prove his own wholehearted, enthusiastic, voluntary commitment to the task of apostolic preaching to which he has been called, that he chooses to abandon one of his rights. He turns his back on his right to be supported, knowing that this decision will cost him an enormous amount of additional time, effort, labor, and misunderstanding. But it will enable him to preach the gospel "free of charge" and thus model the freedom of grace by the way he serves. It will also enable him to show that he serves, not merely out of compulsion, but out of a transformed mind and will, so that by God's grace he is in fact laying up treasure in heaven.

What a refreshing attitude! What a deeply Christian perspective! Many ministers of the gospel today are very concerned about salary levels and benefits packages. Certainly such matters have to be sorted out. But Paul is more concerned to demonstrate that he ministers out of a transformed will—out of a passion to serve, not out of a begrudging compulsion. And if the only way he can demonstrate this commitment is by abandoning some of his rights, so be it; Paul will cheerfully abandon them.

This is the point where Paul begins the first paragraph I cited at the head of this chapter: "Though I am free and belong to no man, I make myself a slave to everyone, to win as many as possible" (9:19). While the Corinthians were despising Paul for his failure to charge a good fee, Paul was delighting in his principled self-denial. In fact, he says, this approach to his ministry affects far more than finance. It touches all his decisions. Because he knows who he is as a Christian, he is free and belongs to no one; at the same time, he voluntarily chooses to make himself a slave of everyone.

Thus Paul's personal example has an enormous bearing on the relatively minor question raised in 1 Corinthians 8, the question as to whether Christians should eat meat that had been offered to idols. That is probably why, in this paragraph, Paul not only says things like "To the Jews I became like a Jew, to win the Jews," and "To those not having the law I became like one not having the law," but also "To the weak I became weak, to win the weak" (9:20–22). He is harking back to his earlier discussion about weak Christians. But the fact of the matter is that Paul's example extends far beyond the issue of meat offered to idols. It has become his lifestyle; it is the working out in one extraordinary life of what it means to take up your cross and follow Jesus. It is a demonstration of what it means to be a world Christian.

We must not stand on our rights. As long as defending our rights remains the lodestar that orders our priorities, we cannot follow the way of the cross.

This sort of self-denial is easy enough to admire in other believers. One can formulate all sorts of interesting theological lessons deriving from Paul's treatment of what to do about meat that has been offered to idols. But the power of this position of principle becomes obvious only when we are called upon to abandon *our* rights.

Even in the home, many arguments are nourished because neither side wants to give up a point. We fight to protect our rights. But I suspect that some of the most trying tests of our preparedness to give up our rights occur when we are thrust into multicultural circumstances for a while. Little things can prove very irritating. When I have chaired seminars that include Christian thinkers from around the world, not a little of my energy has been devoted to trying to read the different cultural signals. From the moment participants first enter the room, the cultural differences are apparent. The Latins arrive, and there are kisses all around. A German shows up, and he has to shake everyone's hand. Hispanics want to stand about eighteen inches from you when you converse together; Anglo-Saxons prefer something closer to a yard. To the Anglos, the Hispanics appear pushy and uncouth; to the Hispanics, the Anglos, who are constantly backing up, are distant and unfriendly and are putting on airs of superiority. The Japanese enter and bob their heads. The American member saunters in and remarks loudly, "Hi, everybody. Sorry I'm late!" He is late—by about ten minutes. But he will not understand what "late" really looks like until the Africans arrive.

Somewhere in the discussion, the Japanese scholar makes what he feels is a very telling and powerful point: "Do you think, brothers, that it might be possible for us to consider looking at this another way?" After he has finished his softly spoken and understated suggestion, the Norwegian dismisses him: "That cannot be! That is not what the passage means at all!" The Japanese is cowed into silence for the next two hours, wondering what kind of barbarians he has encountered. Half of the rest of the members think the Japanese scholar is rather timid.

It's all great fun when it only lasts for a few days. But months and months of a new culture can be very wearing. And in a sense, that is what is going on even within America, or any other Western industrialized country. The pace of change is so fast that different generations are clashing with each other almost like competing cultures. For example, the radically different tastes in music that divide many congregations at the moment are, in part, culture clashes. And it is not easy to be wise. Some wag has said that the last seven words of the church will be, "We've always done it this way before." On the other hand, I have some sympathy for the position of C. S. Lewis, who maintained that he could put up with almost any pattern of corporate worship, so long as it did not change too often. His point is that mere novelty is in fact distracting. The deepest and best corporate worship takes place when the forms are so familiar you never see them and can penetrate the reality. But try explaining *that* at your next church meeting.

Ultimately, there can never be peace and progress on these and many related matters unless all sides carefully listen to the others and humbly resolve, while making a case, never to stand on their own rights. That is the way of the cross. It is the very lifeblood of those involved in cross-cultural outreach—and increasingly, that means all of us!

We Must Adopt as Our Aim the Salvation of Men and Women

Paul repeatedly makes this point. "I make myself a slave to everyone," he writes, "to win as many as possible" (9:19). "To the Jews I became like a Jew, *to win* the Jews" (9:20, emphasis added). "To the weak I became weak, *to win* the weak" (9:22, emphasis added). And this: "I have become all things to all men so tha*t by all possible means I might save some*" (9:22, emphasis added). At the end of the entire section, the same thought is still on Paul's mind: "So whether you eat or drink or whatever you do, do it all for the glory of God. Do not cause anyone to stumble, whether Jews, Greeks, or the church of God—even as I try to please everybody in every way. For I am not seeking my own good but the good of many, *so that they may be saved*. Follow my example, as I follow the example of Christ" (10:31–11:1, emphasis added).

This aim, repeated by the apostle in order to underline its importance, has the effect of focusing and even limiting some of the other principles he articulates. I shall sketch two areas where this is so.

First, although under the last point I summarized much of Paul's thought in these chapters under the slogan, "We must not stand on our rights," in fact that slogan needs qualifying. I thought it best to set the words out in stark power first; the fact remains that the slogan is slightly misleading. If the aim of the exercise were merely not to stand on our rights, then it would always be mandated of us not to stand on our rights. We would become the most amazing conglomeration of wimps. But in fact Paul himself, who could talk so much about self-denial and about

not insisting on his rights, sometimes made much of them. On
more than one occasion, for instance, he appealed to his Roman
citizenship to escape a beating. Was he not simply standing on
his rights?

But Paul is not interested in setting aside his rights as an end
in itself. "I make myself a slave to everyone," he points out, "*to
win as many as possible*" (9:19, emphasis added). If no one's spiritual well-being will be threatened if he eats meat, doubtless he
will order a steak. Paul takes his beatings from the Jewish synagogue; in some instances where he is about to be beaten by the
Romans, however, Paul raises before the Roman authorities the
question of his legal standing as a Roman citizen. He does so precisely because he is interested in establishing legal precedents
that will protect the church. Certainly that is Luke's reading of
events in the Book of Acts. Luke carefully records decision after
decision issued in favor of the nascent Christian movement. He
wants this accumulation of legal precedents to help protect the
church. In other words, Paul is still acting out of a deep principle:
he wants to win as many as possible. In some instances, standing
on one's rights may be exactly what is called for. Yet one should
always be ready to abandon the appeal to one's rights. Precisely
which is the wisest course of action in a particular crisis may
largely be determined by this question about the aim and effect
of the options: How will this course of action contribute to, or
hinder, the work of the gospel?

Second, from the perspective of the broad theme of this chapter, it is important to recognize that becoming a world Christian
cannot be an end in itself. The aim is not to become so international and culturally flexible that one does *not* fit in anywhere;
the aim, rather, is to become so understanding and flexible that
one *can* soon fit in and further the gospel anywhere.

That is a lesson I have had to learn the hard way. When I first
returned home to Canada after an initial stint overseas of three
years, I returned to the metropolitan area where I had previously
served as a pastor. I brought my bride with me, a young English-
woman who had never lived outside England. We found the
church scene deeply depressing. In order to introduce her to the
area, I took her to several different churches over the first few
weeks we were in the country, and each exposure was worse than

the previous ones. I found the people and the churches parochial, narrow, ill-informed, and so on. I provided almost no emotional support to my wife in her attempt to adapt to a new culture.

One Sunday evening, after six weeks or two months had elapsed, I said to my wife, "Come on. Tonight we'll slip out of town, a little farther afield, to a church I know where the pastor is a serious minister of the Word. Let's go there tonight." But as it happened, the regular minister was not speaking that night. There was a guest preacher from New York, who thundered away about the evils of communism. His repeated line, drummed home in a high-pitched, nasal, New York twang, was (and I quote), "The fight against communism is the fight for God." My wife and I walked out.

It took me almost six months before I could look at myself in the mirror and give myself a good scolding. "Carson, you hypocritical idiot. If the Lord called you to Jamaica or Japan, to Mauritius or Mombasa, you would cope. You would discipline yourself to understand the culture and the people and would learn to minister within that framework. Are you so arrogant that you cannot make the same adjustments when you return to your own people? Can you not see that it is not they who have changed, but you? Do you despise them because they have not enjoyed the breadth of cultural exposure in different countries that you have experienced?" So in the Lord's mercy, I finally settled down.

Since then, I have learned that reverse culture shock is the worst culture shock. Many people who go abroad for a few years brace themselves to handle the new culture; they almost never brace themselves to handle the jarring impact of reentry into the culture they have left behind. At the seminary where I teach, we constantly warn international students of the kinds of reverse culture shock they must expect to face when they return home.

This sort of disorientation also accounts, in part, for the frequency and intensity of the criticism of Western institutions and churches uttered by many "Third World" leaders. God knows there is enough to criticize in the West. Nevertheless, in my experience, very few "Third World" leaders spend much time criticizing the West and stressing the need for properly contextualized theology *until they have spent a few years studying in the West.*

Many, many of them no longer quite fit back home. Meanwhile, where have they learned their criticisms of the West? In the West, of course! To criticize the West is an extremely Western thing to do. In fact, to criticize wherever we are is an extremely Western thing to do. Very few of these leaders, for whatever reason, actually engage in much contextualized theology. Instead, they make their reputations criticizing the West.

Of course, I have met some wonderful exceptions to all these generalities. But the generalities ring true to many who have traveled in Christian circles in different parts of the world.

All of this criticism would change its face considerably if the aim were always "to win as many as possible." So much of the awkwardness of not quite fitting in anywhere would disappear, if we simply chose to act in such a way as to accomplish this aim.

The more that a gap opens up between the culture of the church and the culture of the surrounding society, the more important it is to know how to bridge that gap. But the concern must never be to prove how cosmopolitan and sophisticated and flexible we are. The aim must always be "to win as many as possible."

Certainly it is easy to recall instances where that was not the aim! A friend of mine, a minister at a church in England, was asked to go up to Scotland and speak at a mission sponsored by a Christian group in a Scottish university. Astonishingly, though they had been expecting about 75 people to show up the first night, 150 turned out—half of them Muslims who had decided to come as a group to find out for themselves what Christians thought. The Christians in the university thought they needed to "warm up" the crowd, so they produced a singing group that went through a number of Scottish ballads. Since half of those ballads took potshots at the English, this went down very well, especially with my friend sitting there. Then this musical group, bright eyed and bushy tailed, announced they would like to sing some Christian songs. They began with (Can you believe it?) "Awake! Awake! O Zion/Come clothe yourself with strength"— and 75 Muslims walked out.

One must not be too hard on those young Scottish Christians. They simply did not think. But that is a tragedy in itself. They never carefully asked the question, "What should I do *to win as many as possible?*" At least they did not call their mission a *crusade*! That word does not fly very high in Muslim circles.

Barriers must be overcome. Different groups have different languages, smells, tolerances, history, shared memory. Some groups deploy quite an individual sense of humor. It took me three or four days, the first time I lectured in Australia, to appreciate that the warmest introductions were the most scathing, as Australians often indulge in their national pastime of "cutting down the tall poppy." Different financial strata must be crossed. In some countries, England for example, the gospel has moved almost entirely in middle- and upper-middle-class strata. To appreciate the historical reasons how this came about does not itself address the fact that the blue-collar worker is almost untouched by the gospel in that country.

We must adopt as our aim the salvation of men and women. That vision will enable us to avoid cloister Christianity. We need to meditate on Psalms 96 and 98; Isaiah 49:1–13; Jeremiah 12:12–17; Micah 4; Colossians 1:15–29; and Revelation 4–5. We must become global in our awareness and compassion. Cultural sensitivity and flexibility must become tools to enable us to address the challenges of cross-cultural evangelism wisely and courageously, rather than ends in themselves to create a myopic elite of lovely, flexible people.

We Must Recognize That This Stance Is Bound Up with Our Own Salvation

That is the rather staggering conclusion to which Paul arrives in verse 23: "I do all this for the sake of the gospel," he writes, "that I may share in its blessings." We might have expected Paul to write, ". . . that *they* may share in its blessings." But that is not what he says. Paul takes all of the steps outlined in our chapter, and commits himself to such rigorous self-denial, for the sake of the gospel, that *he* might share in its blessings. What does he mean?

If I understand him aright, he is saying that he cannot conceive of any other way of being a Christian. He acts this way to promote the gospel, and that surely means his actions will be for the good of his hearers. But to follow the crucified Messiah means Paul must take up his own cross daily, die to self-interest, and serve the One who bought him. One cannot properly promote the gospel any other way. To promote it this way—by dying to self-interest, giving up all insistence upon the sacredness of one's rights, and striving to win as many as possible—is to follow Christ crucified, who died, literally, to *his* self-interest, gave up all insistence upon the sacredness of *his* very real rights, and set himself to win men and women from every people and tongue and tribe and nation. There is no other way of following Christ; there is no other way of sharing in the gospel's blessings.

That is the point of the closing paragraph of 1 Corinthians 9. Using athletic metaphors, running and boxing, Paul exhorts the Corinthian believers to run the Christian race and to fight the Christian fight in such a way as to get the prize. That means, as it does for the Olympian, self-discipline, self-denial, and strict training. That is the kind of discipline Paul has imposed on himself; it is what he expects every Christian to adopt. Absurd shadowboxing or a pleasant meandering stroll through the meadows, while the serious people are pounding down the track, never won anyone a prize. Paul himself would be disqualified if he left the race to pick petunias. The real Christian, by definition, is one who perseveres (e.g., John 8:31; Col. 1:21–23; Heb. 3:14; 2 John 9). For Paul, such perseverance is tied to his ministry. In other words, he does all this for the sake of the gospel, so that *he* may share in its blessings.

Of course, no one will suggest that every Christian must serve the Lord Christ exactly as Paul did. But Paul wants the Corinthian Christians to have the same self-denying attitude that he has displayed. For him, this is not an optional extra; it is bound up with what it means to be a Christian. The "strong" believer who insists on his or her rights is, finally, sinning against Christ (8:12). In principle, so also is anyone who does not grow in the commitment "to win as many as possible" by following the way of the cross.

That means, at the end of the day, that every Christian ought to be a world Christian. My introduction to this chapter was slightly misleading. It might have been taken to mean that there are two kinds of Christians: world Christians and all the others. But Paul sees anything less than a world Christian, in the sense defined in this chapter, as subnormal. Where there is a failure in discipleship, where there is sin against Christ, where there is persistent refusal to follow Paul as he follows Christ in the way of the cross, there too we find an aimless meandering. And if you meander aimlessly when you should be running for the prize, you will be disqualified.

"Run in such a way as to get the prize. Everyone who competes in the games goes into strict training. They do it to get a crown that will not last; but we do it to get a crown that will last forever" (9:24–25).

Questions for Review and Reflection

1. What is a "world Christian"?
2. Why is it important to know who you are *as a Christian*? How does such self-understanding come about?
3. What "rights" have you given up for the sake of the gospel? What rights are you prepared to give up?
4. How does the concern "to win as many as possible" shape your life? Be specific. What can you do to improve in this area?
5. In your own words, explain how the message of the crucified Messiah is tied to what it means to be a world Christian.

Donald A. Carson is research professor of New Testament at Trinity Evangelical Divinity School in Deerfield, Illinois. He has been at Trinity since 1978.

Carson came to Trinity from the faculty of Northwest Baptist Theological Seminary in Vancouver, British Columbia, where he also served for two years as academic dean. He has served as assistant pastor and pastor and has done itinerant ministry in Canada and the United Kingdom.

Carson received the Bachelor of Science in chemistry from McGill University, the Master of Divinity from Central Baptist Seminary in Toronto, and the Doctor of Philosophy in New Testament from the University of Cambridge.

Carson has written or edited over forty-five books, including *The Sermon on the Mount* (Baker, 1978), *Exegetical Fallacies* (Baker, 1984), *Matthew* (Zondervan, 1984), *From Triumphalism to Maturity* (Baker, 1984), *Showing the Spirit* (Baker, 1987), *How Long, O Lord? Reflections on Suffering and Evil* (Baker, 1990), *The Gospel According to John* (Eerdmans, 1991), *A Call to Spiritual Reformation* (Baker, 1992), and *New Testament Commentary Survey* (Baker, 1993). His book, *The Gagging of God: Christianity Confronts Pluralism* (Zondervan, 1996), won the 1997 Evangelical Christian Publishers Association Gold Medallion Award in the category "theology and doctrine." He coauthored *An Introduction to the New Testament* (Zondervan, 1991) and other works. His edited works include *It Is Written: Scripture Citing Scripture* (Cambridge University Press, 1988) and *Biblical Greek Language and Linguistics* (Sheffield Academic Press, 1993). Carson occasionally writes and edits with faculty colleague John Woodbridge; together they wrote the novel *Letters Along the Way* (Crossway, 1993) and edited *Scripture and Truth* (Baker, 1992) and *God and Culture* (Eerdmans, 1993).

Carson was founding chair of The GRAMCORD Institute, a research and educational institution designed to develop and promote computer-related tools for Bible research, focusing especially on the original languages. Carson is an active guest lecturer in academic and church settings around the world.

Carson and his wife, Joy, reside in Libertyville, Illinois. They have two children. In his spare time, Carson enjoys reading, hiking, and woodworking.